John Mackenzie

**Thayendanegea**

An historico-military drama

John Mackenzie

**Thayendanegea**
*An historico-military drama*

ISBN/EAN: 9783337203320

Printed in Europe, USA, Canada, Australia, Japan

Cover: Foto ©ninafisch / pixelio.de

More available books at **www.hansebooks.com**

THE FIGURE CROWNING THE PEDESTAL OF
THE BRANT MONUMENT.

# THAYENDANEGEA:

## AN
## HISTORICO-MILITARY DRAMA.

BY J. B. MACKENZIE

MEMBER OF THE ONTARIO HISTORICAL SOCIETY.

AUTHOR OF
"The Six-Nations Indians in Canada."

PRINTED FOR THE AUTHOR BY
WILLIAM BRIGGS
TORONTO
1898

Entered according to Act of the Parliament of Canada, in the year one thousand eight hundred and ninety-eight, by J. B. MACKENZIE, at the Department of Agriculture.

TO THE

## Reverend William Clark, M.A., LL.D.,

*Professor of Mental and Moral Philosophy, in the University of
Trinity College, Toronto:*

WHOSE FRIENDLY ENCOURAGEMENT—

GRACE ACCORDED ONLY AFTER HIS, AN EXPERT'S, SCRUTINY
OF A PORTION OF THE TIMBER BEING USED—

EXTENDED TO THE AUTHOR, WHILST IT WAS AS YET
REPOSING ON THE STOCKS,

EMBOLDENS HIM TO TEST THE SEA-WORTHINESS

OF THE THIN-RIBBED CRAFT, NOW LAUNCHED

ON THE CHOPPY BILLOWS OF LATTER-DAY CRITICISM,

THE DRAMA OF THAYENDANEGEA

IS INSCRIBED.

# PREFACE.

I AVAIL myself of an introduction mainly to record the motives which led me to compose this poem.

I formed the opinion, first, that it was the bounden duty of *someone* to enter the breach, in order to rid the situation of the singular—not to say affronting—anomaly to be traced through the circumstance of the character and actions of Tecumseh having enlisted the machinery of the drama for their attractive exposition, whilst those of the earlier companion upholder of British supremacy on the continent—one endowed with a many-sided capacity, plainly denied to the other (barely his compeer even in the way of military distinction) one who acquired equal celebrity for his bearing in the martial camp, beside the Council-fire, and in the field of diplomacy, remain unchapleted by any memorial tribute tendered him of the kind.

I believed, again, that no more efficacious—no more convincing—method of refuting the charges of barbarity freely fabricated by American historians against Brant, could be practised than the bringing in request, so to speak, Thespis' undistorting camera, to imprint a few of those occurrences, which —as a component part of the portraiture designed to be revealed—exhibit him as a foeman who; while ceasing at no time, perhaps, to inspire animosity and dread, was yet, in his treatment of fellow-beings weighed down by affliction and suffering—dragged, under the heart-breaking empire of War, behind the chariot wheels of an adverse fortune—alike generous and humane.

To dispel the suspicion liable withal to be entertained, by those enjoying but cursory acquaintance with his career, that the showing forth of the famous War-captain, in the pages of the drama, exaggerates his eminence—that there has been a fictitious gilding of the plate, an over-adorning of the tapestry—I invoke the estimate of him voiced by the Hon. Ellis H. Roberts, upon an occasion (the centennial observance of Oriskany) well fitted to awake the slumbering resentment of colonials against all such faithful adherents of the Crown: "superior to St. Leger" (the British Commander) "in natural powers and personal magnetism, was Brant—the ideal Indian; with all the genius of his tribe, and the training gained in Connecticut schools, and in the family of Sir William Johnson: among the Indians he was pre-eminent, and in any circle would have been conspicuous;" to fortify which, condensing the conclusion found in Appleton's Cyclopædia, that, "as a warrior, he was cautious, sagacious, and brave; as a diplomat and courtier, adroit and accomplished; while his humanity to a captive or fallen foe is too well established to admit of doubt."

With a life so brimful of stirring and of pregnant adventure such as Brant's, the difficulty of making a selection of incidents, which should at once, with adequacy, typify the man, and interest and divert

the reader, will, I imagine, be frankly recognized.
I can only hope that I have succeeded in presenting
my protagonist as a fairly consistent, rationally
behaved character. I trust, further, that there have
been sketched with a *soupçon*, at all events, of fidelity,
Sir William Johnson, *fidus Achates*—whole-souled, un-
selfish (the scope of the production has not permitted
a dealing, otherwise than by retrospect, with his in-
estimable public services); Colonel Guy Johnson, the
no less devoted believer in, than hot-tempered champion of, Monarchy; Major Butler, the efficient military
commander, and unerring analyst of Indian nature;
Captain Pouchot, the gifted, incorruptible servant of
France; Benedict Arnold—valiant, dare-devil—the
Prince Rupert of the Provincials.

I consider that it would be unfitting for me to
close this preface without the confession that not only
was the matured product given an exceptional chance
to attain a sounder development, a better growth,
through Professor Clark's passing of his critical har-
row over the germinal deposit: these have been
scarcely less advanced through the willing assistance
rendered by Miss Mabel MacLean Helliwell, of the
Ontario Historical Society, in the preparation of the
notes, and in revising the proofs of the verse; all
her suggestions as to the reshaping of which having
served to improve both expression and rhythm.

I have also to thank Mr. James Bain, Jr., for point-
ing me to unsuspected sources of knowledge; Captain
Cruikshank for the loan of MSS. notes; and Mr. J. O.
Brant-Sero for a free imparting of family traditions.

# AUTHOR'S ERRATA.

Page 54, for lines from 353-57 inclusive substitute the following:

"Should the unenvied consignees attempt
To board the fleet of bending *Indiamen*,
Then entering the harbor with their freight,
To land the strifeful cargoes. This the pale,
Uneasy chapmen—venturesome, though scarce" . .

Page 59. In statement of time of scene, for "June" read "July."

Page 92. In announcement of the entrance of characters, for "Captain" read "Captains," and treat the name "Bull"—with the conjunction "and" before it—as though, instead of following, it had preceded, "Canastota."

Page 96, line 547—for "unhurled" read "unproved."

# DRAMATIS PERSONÆ.

THAYENDANEGEA—JOSEPH BRANT: *Sachem of the Mohawks, and Principal War-chief of the Six-Nations; sometime Secretary to* COLONEL GUY JOHNSON.

SIR WILLIAM JOHNSON: *Superintendent of Indian Affairs for the Northern district of North America; Colonel, afterwards Major-General, on the Colonial establishment.*

JOHN BUTLER: *Major, afterwards Colonel, of British quasi-regulars, Commander of "Butler's Rangers"; sometime Interpreter for the Indian department.*

GUY JOHNSON: *Superintendent of Indian Affairs, in succession to* SIR WILLIAM JOHNSON; *Colonel of British Militia.*

CAPTAIN POUCHOT: *Commandant of Fort Niagara, under the French domination; Officer of the Royal Regiment of Béarn.*

CANASTOTA—JOHN MOHAWK: *A subordinate chief of the Mohawks.*

JOHN PRIDEAUX: *Brigadier-General in the British army.*

EYRE MASSEY: *Colonel in the British army.*

SAMPSON SAMMONS: *a yeoman of the Mohawk Valley.*

NICHOLAS HERKIMER: *Brigadier-General of Provincial Militia.*

SIR JOHN JOHNSON: *Son, and successor of* SIR WILLIAM JOHNSON *in the baronetcy; Colonel of "Johnson's Greens."*

JOHN STUART: *Anglican Missionary to the Mohawks.*

BENEDICT ARNOLD: *Major-General, and Commander-in-Chief of the armies of the United States of America on the Mohawk River.*

MARINUS WILLETT: *Colonel of Provincials.*

HON YOST SCHUYLER: *a private soldier in "Butler's Rangers."*

LIEUTENANT BONNAFOUX: *Officer of French artillery, serving under* POUCHOT.

## DRAMATIS PERSONÆ.

KAENDAE : *a chief of the Senecas, attached to the French interest.*

SUSPENDED COLLAR : *a chief of the Onondagas.*

SANGUERACHTA : *a War-chief of the Senecas.*

SIR GUY CARLETON, *Governor of Canada, at the outbreak of the Revolution; and a second time, as* LORD DORCHESTER, *after the pacification.*

EBENEZER COX, ICHABOD ALDEN : *Colonels of Provincials.*

JOHN WOOD : *Major of Provincials.*

JOHN MCKINSTRY : *Captain of Provincials.*

ALEXANDER HARPER : *Lieutenant of Provincials.*

WALTER BUTLER : *Lieutenant, afterwards Captain, in "Butler's Rangers."*

WILLIAM TRYON : *Governor of the Province of New York before the Revolution.*

DAVID HAMBLE : *a yeoman of Cherry Valley.*

JOSEPH WAGGONER : *a soldier serving under* GENERAL HERKIMER.

JOHN VEEDER : *a yeoman of the Mohawk Valley.*

NICHOLAS SCHUYLER : *a yeoman of the Mohawk Valley.*

SUSAN CAMPBELL : *a matron of Cherry Valley.*

ALICE LINDESAY : *a matron of Cherry Valley.*

ELIZABETH SCHUYLER : *a matron of the Mohawk Valley.*

*A* CHIEF *of the* MISSISAKES ; *a* CHIEF *of the* POUTEOTAMIES.

*A Herald from* SIR WILLIAM JOHNSON.

*A* SPOKESMAN *for the* ONONDAGAS.

*A* SPOKESMAN *for the* CAYUGAS.

*A* SPOKESMAN *for* IROQUOIS *women.*

*Mute characters:* VAN CAMPEN, PENCE *and* PIKE, *yeomen of the* MINISINK : ISAAC BRANT, *son of* THAYENDANEGEA ; JONCAIRE-CLAUZONNE, *a Seneca half-breed, attached to the French interest;* CAPTAIN BULL, *a Royalist officer.*

*Officers and soldiers of the* BRITISH, FRENCH *and* PROVINCIAL *armies; couriers, orderlies; Chiefs, warriors and women of the* SIX-NATIONS ; *Chiefs and warriors of divers north-western and south-western tribes.*

# THAYENDANEGEA.

## ACT I.

SCENE 1.—PLACE: *Fort Niagara—Encampment of the British army of investment.*

TIME: *July, 1759.*

*Enter* GENERAL PRIDEAUX.

GEN. PRIDEAUX *(apostrophizing the fort)*:
Of Onguiaahra's tamed, exhausted flood
Thou that abidest sentry respiteless;
Outgazer, thou, absorbed—serene—upon
Ontario's gleaming waste; flagrant the greed—
Th' ambition towering—proud France confessed,
Time when of old proposed she to uprear
Thy sullen fabric! What disclaimer round
Of England's puissance (flower whose splendid prime,
Within these protest-hurling—rather should
I say these grievance-forging—colonies,      10
Sore-menaced is by shrivelling autumn-breath
Of pale decadence) those cold cylinders
 Betimes shall bellow! What contemptuous—

What vaunting—challenge to her governance
(Close-shielding rule, in her own domicile
Full slightingly appraised) each loosening curl
Of the silk-woven banner doth emit!
Ours be it here that ensign—when commenced
The motions on the chess-board—to degrade;
Ours be it *then* those growlers to kennèl!  20
Ours their venomed releasers let it be—
Ours its defiant flaunters—to o'erwhelm!
Yet waiving question overshadowing—
This angle's place as firm-set janitor
Of Nature's burnished pathway to fat-veined
Hesperian tracts—at hand how virtuous
The salve to bring assoilment for its theft!
Verdurous meadow fills the lakeward view—
Cleft by the river's line of mica-braid;
For vivid background, daïssed tier on tier  30
Of stately plateau; whose tressed coronal
Of shaggy spires the taintless ether pricks.
Environs those—the truly marvellous,
Sublime commingling of two elements;
Lodging, I wis—to momently assume
The role vaticinal, Gael's second-sight
Vouchsafed me for the nonce—the quickening germ
Of an Elysium. Novel conceit,
Perhaps, but in its hues essential—chief

Constituents—that aspect in my eyes 40
To tunic worn by rifle-regiments
Affords similitude: the shaven sward
The finished textile forms; appeals the stream
As silvery facing; hirsute epaulets
The dim, presiding wood consents to lend.
But forms approach to break my reverie.—
Oust idle fantasies.

*Enter* THAYENDANEGEA *and* SIR WILLIAM
JOHNSON.

*(To Sir William J.)*

      Thrice-welcome art,
Stout victor of Lake George; who stepp'st at once
(As if by its high memory inspired)
From duty pregnant, function apposite— 50
Formally claiming, through suggestive name,
For Britain's lord those crystal surfaces—
To proudly reach the grander dignity:
Purger auspicious of our storied fame
From th' ignominy—stinging, foul disgrace—
By Braddock's folly-weighted arms sustained
Near Fort Du Quesne—Monongahela's black,
Entombing wave.

 SIR WM. JOHNSON. Called an apprentice, then,
To your world-preaned craft; unversed in War's

Astutely-managed game—disposing shrewd,   60
Strategic of the pawns—my conquest might
Have not been so decisive, had not Fate
Closed an alliance with the conqueror.
He well content had been, I sometimes think,
Of immature exploit to have foregone
The crown—State-lavished title, donatives—
To win the skill, pluck the experience,
That garnered were by you at Dettingen.
Nor without shade of envy might one view
Your fit succession to the colonelcy,   70
Haloed by Howe—the trainèd warrior,
Rude-felled year past in self-same wilds, where I
(Think not the contrast wakes complacency,
The accident gives rise to jubilance)
Before prevailed, the tyro—that pure gem;
As loving, as beloved; soft-nurtured, yet
The fortune poor, scant rations, bivouac
Of humblest unit in the camp partook:
Master profound of warfare's science—lore;
Of whom Wolfe said, "Best soldier of the King—   80
The noblest Englishman that in my time
Appeared." But as you're pleased thus to extol
My services, I bring to you to-day
A youthful zealot in my retinue;
Full hardy sprout, whom first the speeding lead

Did, like myself, on those hushed shores salute ;
Thayendanegea—since the striking down
Before our moistening eyes of valorous
"King" Hendrick—rising hope in fight become
Of the imperial Mohawks, perfect heir       90
To his dropped mantle ; budding Joshua.

   GEN. PRIDEAUX (*to Thayendanegea*).
Aspiring youth, rejoiced am I to find
You so determined, anxious—so afire—
That ardent dedication to confirm
Of fresh-blown, effervescent energies
On grieved and smitten country's altar-fires !

   THAYANDANEGEA (*to Sir William Johnson*).
Speaking of gallant Hendrick, you'll recall
His counsel pressed before th' engagement ; how,
When it was mooted to divide our force,
Dieskau's retirement to break in upon,       100
He proffer made of most sententious speech :
"Too few each party, if required to fight ;
Too numerous, if to be killed instead."
Picking up twigs, with which to illustrate
His sober utterance, he forcibly
Upon them bare ; when supervened at heel
Comment oracular : "together grouped,
These sticks to rend a trial strenuous
Defied ; whereas, if you disjoin them, lo !

Each, by itself, is broken easily." 110
Malign, indeed, th' appearance Fortune wore ;
When she deprived us—not alone of him,
But of that soaring spirit, Ephraim
Williams; whose death the gracious seed inearthed,
To blossom into an academy. [borough's

SIR WM. J. Well I remember. Could a Marl-
Deep foresight have impressed more sound advice?
(*To Gen. P.*) To edify you, Prideaux, I would add
There's warrant questionless for my young friend's
Lauding the maxim taught through that address;
Since in our language his rhythmical name 121
Has "wedded brands" for its equivalent. [concerns

GEN. PRIDEAUX. To pass, my valued colleague, to
Of living, of engrossing interest—
Needs not to say that you already have
With sapient instinct grasped, in all its bold
And stirring magnitude, the present plan
For the unsparing, signal punishment—
For ultimate expulsion—of the French;
Which the Great Minister, with shakeless faith, 130
His armies on this hemisphere hath set
To execute. *Our* men (deserve they not
Guerdon as full as Bradstreet reaped from his
Brisk siege of Frontenac) assault this keep;
Whilst Haldimand—by whom La Corne's blind dash

Has just been foiled—safe holds against surprise
Oswego; Amherst, wielding of brigades
On land engaged the principal command—
Flushed by the brilliant coup himself and his
High-souled right-arm achieved at Louisburg—  140
With leaguering column shall (bent they upon
Retrieving Abercromby's hard reverse)
On scarred Ticonderoga rudely fall;
When, having overcome its garrison—
Dispersed such troops as hasten to their aid—
By glassed Champlain, and jewelled links beyond,
Fares he to old Quebec; uniting there
With Saunders—Wolfe—to wrest the citadel.

   Sir W. J. Far-reaching scheme—reflection faithful,
Of its projector!  Notwithstanding, led  [clear
Am I decidedly to doubt, in view  151
Of leagues despairful that between them lie;
Of checks, of hindrances—impediments—
From snaring evils of the Richelieu;
Its toothèd rocks—those ambushed highwaymen—
Its frilled cascades—the shallows' drapery
Of shining lawn: delays in traversing
The portages, that Amherst there arrives
To launch with Wolfe concerted enterprise.
Moreover, since their simultaneous  160
Mooring before Cape Diamond's beetling front

Cannot occur—one moving from the south,
One up the gulf—Montcalm might seize the chance
To strike the severed squadrons, each in turn.
                          [*Exeunt omnes.*

---

SCENE 2.—PLACE : *Compartment in the Fort.*

*Enter* CAPT. POUCHOT, KAENDAE, *and* JONCAIRE-CLAUZONNE.

CAPT. POUCHOT. The startling proof we've managed
Our adversaries of the blundering     [to afford
Construction of their trenches—by our ruse
Of challenging encounter—that our guns
Sweep their cheap works, will, I feel confident,
Lame the impression that the Iroquois       170
Are wont to harbor of their potency.
These surely cannot relish the device
Of being so stationed that they must attract
The blended fire of shell and musketry
Delivered by our wakeful soldiery.
By dextrous handling, might we not induce
Surrender of their partialities ;
Push our advantage, haply, to relieve       178
Them of a share of the Sonnontouans.     [them.
    KAENDAE. With your permission, I will talk to

Capt. P. Granted's my leave to undertake the parle.
[*Exit* Kaendae.
If we could but detach these warriors;            182
Who from their numbers (I would place the count
At full nine hundred) superadd to which
Their wide acquaintance with the vicinage,
Source are to me of more uneasiness
Than all the arts of their confederates,
From Prideaux' force, it would so cripple him
That he terms for a peace might entertain.
Had we not these auxiliaries, moreo'er,            190
To reckon with, not vainly might we hope
The faulty fosses of the enemy
To render still more futile—nay—destroy.

[*Hailing a Sergeant*]
Should legates from th' opposing Iroquois,
On his return, accompany our chief;
See that they carefully blindfolded are,
'Fore they have access to the inner fort.

(Kaendae *is here observed before the walls, with two Indians. He accosts the commandant.*)

Kaendae. Wait with me chieftains of the
Commissioned by them as an embassy      [Iroquois;
To treat with you. While craving audience;    200
Insist do they on pledge, ere entering
Your chambers dull—the word of Joncaire, whom

2

They've always classed among their family,
Would ease their doubts—for their immunity
From harmful usage ; from being jeoparded
By methods underhand.  Will you extend
To them such grace—engage to that effect ?
    CAPT. P.  Joncaire is here.  Safe-conduct is decreed.

(KAENDAE *now enters the apartment with the chiefs,
whose eyes are found to be closely bandaged.*)

    [*Re-hailing Sergeant.*]

Relieve the strangers of their bandages ;
That being effected—from the room retire.      210
    IROQUOIS CHIEF.  Our several lodges, cousin,
Adoption by you of too harsh surmise    [deprecate
Concerning motives that impel them now
T' uplift the axe against old comrades.  We,
With candor—prickings e'en of shame—avow
Ourselves unable reason to assign
Adequate—just—for our hostility ;
Plead we, in main, that Johnson ; all intent
To warn us from a falling edifice
(So preyed he on unarmored innocence,      220
Limp wills conforming on his anvil's block)
Our minds infected with the drear belief
That France's glory from its zenith sinks ;
Recedes her might as Ocean's ebbing tide.

Capt. P. Your course, I'm bound to say, creates in
No fleeting wonderment. Friends, what excuse [me
For quarrel had I furnished? Were you here
Contending *for* me—that far worthier step.
Did I not battle for you frequently;
In your behoof employ each faculty;                 230
Strength, will, exerting to humiliate
The strutting nation, which now condescend,
Feigning esteem, to stroke—caress—you? Is
The cloven foot not thinly shrouded; they,
Revivers of that hoar imposture wreaked—
In all its patternless audacity,
With no abatement of its craftiness—
The hungry depredator of the flock
His inroad consummating in a garb
Deceptive? Friends, aforetime had we not        240
Custodians been of one another's trust—
Sharers of one another's warm regard?
When aimed I to abuse your confidence;
Of your respect how earned a forfeiture?
Did not your urbane people me baptize
(Found you the title by one act belied?)
The gushing fount of prodigality?
Reviewed that era of amenities—
Thrown on me now huge burden of distress
(My wont, you've learnt, is not to spare my foes) 250

Through the necessity I find to point
My engines of destruction upon men
Other than our traditional enemies.
Lastly—as ground of all most obvious
Why you no further should embroil yourselves
In this malignant difference—I would
Your heedfullest attention draw to this
Important fact; your kindred from the south—
As from the west—to our assistance move.    259
Are you prepared your clansmen's blood to shed?
If not—break through the English thongs; and, if
You can't be influenced to side with us,
Preserve, at least, fitting neutrality.

(*Here the Commandant presents a collar to the chiefs.*)

This collar carry to your warriors;
'Twill seal my speech with authenticity.

Chief of the Missisakes (*addressing the envoys*).

Brothers, we do congratulate ourselves
That we conduced, in measure, to secure
This sage debate.  We trust it may result
In leading you again to clasp the hand—
Dwell in the sight—of our Great Father; who   270
Has stood by us with spouse-like constancy;
For whom die would we freely—cheerfully.

CHIEF OF THE POUTEOTAMIES (*addressing the envoys*).

Has not, my uncles, the "Master of Life"
Us in this bowery "Isle" deposited;
With orders to his vizier to adhere?
Calls such adhesion for apology?
Were we not, chiefs, the first to brandish blade
In his support; whose bosom yearns for you?
When was evinced more spirit or more pluck—
Determination—than our ancestors'?       280
My uncles! we, with unfeigned pleasure, note
That you from friends' proposals have not shrunk:
We labor to reclaim you from those fiends
Of English (race we know but to abhor)
Repeating wish of these our relatives
That you may once more, kinsmen, come to lean
Our Father's arm upon; for we are loth
Either of ye, our patrons, to forsake.

IROQUOIS CHIEF (*to Capt. Pouchot*).

We will immediately convey to our
Companions all that has been said: expect     290
Our answer by the next meridian.
                    [*Exeunt omnes.*

SCENE 3.—PLACE: *The same.*

*Enter* CAPT. POUCHOT, LIEUT. BONNAFOUX *and* KAENDAE, *followed by a number of Indian women.*

KAENDAE (*to Pouchot*).
The hour assigned for sending their reply
To the pour-parler has elapsed without
Communication forwarded to us
From Johnson's Iroquois; address I now
My prayer for leave to ascertain the cause.
    CAPT. P. You may go forth; but the negotiants,
Through you, are notified that I shall not
The loosing of our missiles on the foe
Suspend; since I, by reconnoitring close      300
The scene, have just discovered that he used
Th' extended period of our discourse
His works to expedite perceptibly.
Take with you, then, this pole-tacked banneret;
It you can hoist, in case the deputies
Solicit readmission to the fort.
    KAENDAE. Such your behest I'll studiously obey.
                      [*Exit* KAENDAE.

*After a short interval,* KAENDAE *reappears before the walls, accompanied by* SUSPENDED COLLAR, *an Onondaga chief, and two Cayugas. The requirement of bandaging the ambassadors' eyes having been fulfilled in this case also, all are admitted; after which the bandages are removed. The chiefs preface discussion by reciprocating the Commandant's gift to the original envoys; tendering him a large white collar, as a symbol of peace.*

 SUSP. C. Cousin, we were beset by obstacles
Placed in our path by Johnson to defeat
Our purpose. This acquits us of designed   310
Remissness. We decision quickly reached
To hold aloof; we leave the English now—
Our birchen cabins on the farther bank—
La Belle Famille to occupy; there massed,
Shall constitute force unattached. Thanks take
For the advice which has persuaded us.
 CAPT. POUCHOT. Your half-loaf, chieftain, we full
Appropriate.           [gratefully

 (SUSPENDED COLLAR *here presents a string of wampum to* POUCHOT.)

 SUSPENDED COLLAR. Prefer we, though, request
That those the women—children—of our kind;
Since was in ashes laid the Chabert hold,   320

Welcomed by you as wards within the fort,
(That they from shattering bombs might scatheless be
Preserved) should, with Kaendaé, their staff,
Tarry with us at our sequestered camp.
 Capt. P. All these are present. They full liberty
Possess to act as they themselves prescribe;
Albeit, chief, Kaendaé assured
Monsieur Chabert that he would not depart.
Still, I would have no person hesitate.

 (*Here* Kaendae, *in vouchsafing no reply, tacitly affirms what has been recalled to his notice by this remark of the Commandant. The latter—turning now to the women—produces, and spreads before him, the belt and equipment—as figuring a precaution taken against threatened disaster—placed with the dead body of an Indian in the tomb.*)

Witness, frail branches of the Iroquois,   330
(The symbolism all will comprehend)
How to your welfare I devote myself!
Trappings are these which, you're aware, descend
With the stilled body to the noisome grave.
Straightway to death, then, without vengeance owed—
Condignest doom—pray I to be consigned,
If in my charge you meet calamity.

(*The women offer, in recognition, strings to* POUCHOT.)

SPOKESMAN.  Confiding, Sieur, in your integrity,
Declare we, by this sign, our preference
For resting safe-immured within the fort.                340

(*At this stage* SUSPENDED COLLAR *presents an
additional string to the Commandant.*)

Present we token for the Moraiguns;
With the petition that the Outaouais
Have option, likewise, to betake themselves
To near retreat where we our wigwams pitch.

CAPT. POUCHOT (*aside to Lieut. Bonnafoux*).
This a manœuvre is—to me it smells
So strongly of deceit—inspired, I fear,
By Johnson to incense the Outaouais.
For does it not impute to us—that cool
Demand—suspicion of the faithfulness
Of braves who never wandered from our side?     350

LIEUT. BONNAFOUX (*aside to Capt. Pouchot*).
I would with you conjecture that the piece
By brush was colored of hypocrisy;
Agree with the suggestion that the move
Contributes to a fraudful masquerade,
Which that rare counterfeiter has
Contrived for our peculiar benefit.

CAPT. POUCHOT (*to Suspended Collar*).

Astonished am I not a little, chief,
That band, not e'er as kin acknowledging
The Outaouais, should seek to modify
Their attitude.   Banish fond fallacies!        360
No palterers the Outaouais; disdain
Would they thus to insult the speckless arms;
Damage the high—the sacred—cause of France.

SUSP. C.   We table, Sieur, this tasty edible:
Doughty Kaendaé, short while before
Escorting us through this webbed labyrinth,
Did Johnson's tent fearlessly penetrate.
There come—tossed ceremony to the winds—
The sachem's voice rang in reproach of his
Finesse; pulling the wool over our eyes;      370
Scarified him for his inveigling us
Into this emprise.

KAENDAE.     Bred grim irony;
Johnson the blast imbibed as pleasantry.   [stance;

"S. C."   Closing, we would impress this circum-
We do not make our stand conditional
On your conceding the indulgences;
For which we made request with diffidence;
Our promise given not to incommode
Assailed—assailants—we shall implement.

Capt. Pouchot (*to the envoys*).

Look that your oath be not transgressed. With this ;
There being no longer dart to elevate—       381
Pass—on our controversial battledores,
Dissolved becomes our fruitful conference.
Tickle I would, though, palate of the flesh,
By herewith handing for your separate
Consumption, chiefs, a porous slice of bread—
Largess from decent oven—inasmuch
As I have heard Prideaux allots to you
Far from invigorating dietary—       389
Teeth-plaguing scones beneath the embers baked.

(*The Commandant here suits his action to the word, by portioning to each of the deputies a comfortable dole of bread.*)

[*Exeunt omnes.*

SCENE 4.—Place : *Before the walls of the Fort.*

The batteries renew their attack upon the walls; suspended for a considerable time through need for reconstruction of the original approaches, which, as located, had been found to expose the workers about them too freely to the defenders' fire. In course of the bombardment, so recommenced, one of the cohorns explodes, instantly killing GENERAL PRIDEAUX.

Sir Wm. Johnson (*to officers of the staff*).
Trist offspring of mischance—or of neglect    390
The forfeit burdensome,—which harshly veils
For us a light of gathering brilliancy;
Which snapped the life of gifted officer;
Which closed the race of sterling patriot!
Still must we not, by that fell stroke unnerved,
Relax—suspend—desire; still must we not,
Cowed feebly by disaster, labor spare,
To gain the stronghold.
  [*To an aide-de-camp.*] Bid the cannoneers,
Whiles they redouble, to point true, their fire.
Pray that success remedial eschar spread    400
O'er grim miscarriage; that renown erect
Its eyrie, cloud-envelopèd, from out
The wreck of shuddering fatality!

(*The assault thenceforward is prosecuted amain,
until a number of ugly, scattered rents appear in the
walls. At this juncture, a herald advances to the
battlements, under cover of a flag of truce.*)

HERALD. The mouthpiece am I, worthy castellan,
Of greeting weighty from our General;
His mettled troops—ranks which, you know, comprise
A restive host of qualmless savages;
Whose passions it will be most difficult
To hold in check, if lingers their reprieve     410
From tame inaction in this narrow coign,
Th' embarrassed fort enclose on every side.
Our batteries belch bane, alike from here,
And from the river's western brink; you see
The mischief worked upon the bastions—
The gaping apertures ploughed in your walls;
Our pickets guard (that channel of relief
Debarring) lake-approaches—they patrol
Its bluffs with pauseless vigil—truths that must
Have been to you brought home, with no less clear
Than awkward force, when beaten back by us   421
But yesterday your venturous galley was,
From Cadaraqui's isle-unlocking strait
Wafted with reinforcements. Hoped-for aid
By landward routes a powerful reserve
Stand charged to intercept. Wherefore, to stay

This bloodshed—added horrors 'scape—you are,
In amity, invited to transfer
To us the fastness; its defenders—stores.   [bear:

CAPT. POUCHOT. My flaming cartel to your leader
Quarried by me and hewn, upraised by me           430
The stubborn granite of the sconce—as changed,
Improved, renewed it darks the sky—which now
Enfolds me; graved are earnest, deep resolve—
Exacting toil—upon its lines untrimmed;
Burned in its rugged angles all my faith,
Zeal—loyalty—to France. I cannot—will
Not—yield it.

HERALD.        On your head the consequence!

HERALD *here withdraws; and the siege is continued with undiminished vigor.*

SCENE 5.—PLACE: *Tent of the Commanding General.*

*To* SIR WM. JOHNSON *enter a* COURIER.

COURIER. The foeman's levies, motley armament—
In part, from Erie's southern edge, the rest,
From untracked cantons by the Illinois,          440
Ohio's, marge recruited; whose advance
'Twas laid on me with watchful eye to note—
Instant report; their bateaux beached off Ile

De Marine, push, by Aubry captained and
De Ligneris, to Pouchot's succor.  They,
Ere this, I dare avouch, have come abreast
The cataract.

    Sir Wm. Johnson.  To urgent conference
Quick summon Colonel Massey; say I would
Some wise, effective ordering of our force
With him devise 'gainst battle's imminence.    450
                                [*Exit* Courier.
Since it would but our hard-won vantage sell
To send detachments forth th' invaders' use
Of the flint-paven portage to dispute;
Heralds their march a struggle desperate
In the parched open for the mastery:
Suspended soon in trembling balances
Glory, dishonor; triumph and defeat!
Build should we on the looser discipline
Of our opponents, now, our surest ground
Of trust; on tactics draw to combat force.    460

    (*Enter* Colonel Massey.)

I begged your presence, Massey, to discuss
With you at large the hour's emergency;
On it I do invoke your spoken mind—
Beseech your candid thought—that judgment crave,
To which your training on the elder sod

Lends rarest value.  My opinion hear :
The portage-outlet has (De Lancey proved
His competence) been strongly fortified :
It let us treat, then, as the *point d'appui ;*
There—since the mob, hard-visaged and unkempt
(A compost curious of nondescripts) 471
Have here enrolled among them, 'tis announced,
Surprising marksmen from the outer posts—
There should the Province's light infantry,
A smaller number of the Grenadiers,—
With a proportion of your regulars—
Station assume behind the abattis :
On either flank bestowed—these, after all,
Failed Pouchot to estrange—the Indians
(Sage Butler for their head—as subaltern 480
Thayendanegea—would I nominate)
Less hampered in this posture they would be
With fiery onsets they might meditate.

 Col. Massey.  Chime well the measures you thus
With my conceptions.     [briefly sketch
 Sir Wm. Johnson.  Let me signify
Reliance on your skill, activity—
Your wisdom, well-approved capacity—
By leaving, without scruple, in your hands
Their charge supreme, their full accomplishment.
As to the new-arrived belligerents— 490

Somewhat disquieted am I by word
Of Western braves being found in Aubry's ranks;
Some owning consanguinity with those
That feed our muster.  To the foe's bleak fold
Lured such have been by sundry blandishments,—
The viscid slime of meddling Jesuits;
In province secular, salivous snakes
Which one *might* hope to scotch, though not to kill;
(Monitions, preaching; piety of these
To measure cat of Bourbon interests)  500
Dissembling clerics, oily cozeners;
Such as infest the central Carrying Place;
Whose sleights it irks King George to neutralize—
At war the toxic with the antidote;
By artful droppings of sinistrous hints
Of attitude to be by us employed,
To this proud race's grievous detriment;
Of policy with hate to be pursued—
Filching of lands, throttling of liberties;
Enforced removal from their settlements—  510
Should our emergence from the deathful mill,
Which this stern wrestle goes to institute,
Be, in the end, propitious.  To so marked
Extent the nature of the redman's made
A harbourage for veering impulses,—
So close is modelled on the weathervane—

I fear, lest, parleys opening with our bands
(We've seen how accurately Pouchot gauged
Their tendency to traffic with their trust)
The spigot fly from their cooped fealty.                520
   Col. M.  Direction of so large a following
Of the Six-Nations as encamp with us;
Point that induced me, when brave Prideaux fell,
To waive my title to the leadership;
While you stood there, of all best qualified
To hold them well-affected to the cause;
Which they, 'twas said, had none too willingly
Espoused—were serving with half-heartedness.
Returning to the sphere of strategy,—
Whilst I th' assigned divisions shall conduct,        530
Attack thus plainly threatened to resist;
You will, in your wise superintendency,
Protect, I'm sure, the trenches; keeping there
A fair-sized company of our array,
To cope with sorties from the garrison:
Behoves, as well, contingent to detail
Projects to baffle for abrupt descent
Upon the transports—passage so preserve,
In case of hopeless worsting, for retreat.
                                    [*Exeunt.*

SCENE 6.—PLACE: *Building of the Fort—Bastion of the Five-Nations.*

*Enter* CAPT. POUCHOT *and* LIEUT. BONNAFOUX.

CAPT. POUCHOT (*gazing through an embrasure towards the wood*).

To lighten mind long fretted by suspense—   540
For lead-shooned week Doubt's joyless intimate,
Grown has the ridge to my intensive sight
A haunt at last of human tenancy;
Distinguish do I now compacted rows—
Figures whose sensile armature gives back
The sun's rich splendor; Aubry's vanguard, they.

  LIEUT. B. Our brief advice gave the intelligence
That he conducts a strange-assorted crew.

  CAPT. P. Granting such news to be correct; with
Attend a corps of expert riflemen—   [him
Inured each one of them to border broils—   551
The bushmen from recesses of Presqu' Ile;
Sharp-shooters from Fort Machault and Le Bœuf.
Further, both Aubry and De Ligneris
Are so adroit—efficient—that they're bound
To drive these English hornets to their boats.

  (*Brisk firing is now heard from the direction of the*

*clearing, mingled with the strident war-whoops of
Indians.*)

While forced upon our ears those volleys sharp—
The knell, belike, of loved compatriots—
How would you, Bonnafoux, the fact explain,
That for sustainèd interval has ceased     560
To rain upon us the besiegers' fire;
Where probe for secret of that grateful lull
In their attentions!

   LIEUT. BONNAFOUX. I would fancy those
Deputed for the more exhaustive task
Of razing these gray battlements were sent
To swell their army's numbers in the field.

   CAPT. P. Th' occasion's suitable, if that be so,
To risk a sally. Do you, then, instruct
De Villars to collect, in furtherance
Of such design, good moiety of our     570
Defenders; let him be enjoined to feel
His way; great prudence practise—watchfulness.
                           [*Exit* BONNAFOUX.

*A respectable section of the garrison having been
got together, they sally forth; but have not proceeded
further than the covered way, when a body of men
rise—as if by magic—from concealment in the trenches;
and compel them to withdraw incontinently within
their defences.*

SCENE 7.—PLACE: *The besiegers' trenches.*

SIR WM. JOHNSON (*addressing the retiring French*).

All too deficient, shallow reasoners,
Could you conceive us to be imbeciles;
Prepared to wilfully desert our ground,
And let you cast yourselves in Aubry's arms?
Bide in your battered towers for short-lived term
We grant you, of our grace, their custody;
Cling to your crumbling shelter, till we haste,
From Aubry's overthrow, to end this strife.     580
                    [*Exit* SIR WM. JOHNSON.

---

SCENE 8.—PLACE: *Building of the Fort—Bastion of the Five-Nations.*

*To* CAPT. POUCHOT *enter a* FRENCH INDIAN RUNNER.

RUNNER.   Woe! woe! the hour; the French have
    given way;
And Butler's Mohawks speed their frenzied flight.
   CAPT. P.   I scarce can credit such ill-starred event.
How came our troops so soon demoralized?
   RUNNER.   The foe, concealed by heavy breast-
    works; when

We ventured near them, poured a galling fire;
Then at us rushed at point of bayonet:
Meanwhile, their crouching herd of Indians—
Pegged in the closet of their memory
The lay, each intricacy of the wood— 590
Leapt from its shade, like rolling avalanche;
Falling upon our lines with stress so fierce,
That we became as saplings in a storm.

CAPT. P.  Though hard to live to be thus agonized,
Naught now remains save to resign the fort!

*[Exeunt.*


END OF ACT I.

## ACT II.

SCENE 1.—PLACE: *The Mohawk Valley—Anglican mission-post at Fort Hunter.*

TIME: *Winter of 1771-72.*

*Enter* THAYENDANEGEA *and* REV. JOHN STUART.

THAYENDANEGEA.   Fails oral note to syllable the
  thanks;
Pay ne'er could gratitude, though drained its hoard,
Thou zealous teacher, friendly monitor—
Of Truth the pure-browed, radiant messenger—
For train of love-spurred efforts to promote
My people's inner weal.   Devoted priest,
No early-drooping bays proportioned meed
Of thy staunch travailings; publish not these
The heart-kept tally of thy ministerings:
A delving there—superb self-sacrifice—               10
By whom outdone of school of Loyola?
Feat meritorious enow it were
But to have scratched a long-left fallow soil;
Where skulks fatuity, cowled ignorance;
Fief to which superstition tyrannous
Studies to verify—hastes to defend—
Pre-emptive claim: done nothing more than bid

For the acquest of property, on which
A hide-bound bigotry would fain reserve
Perpetual lien; since laying e'en the fuse,　　20
Whose smart ignition frees the swathèd charge—
The thunderous bolt propels—that hopes, perchance,
To shake—raze—Error's thick-walled donjon, might
The hardiest innovator well perturb,
Most self-reliant propagandist vex.
That prelude in itself full hazardous;
Decrying customs wild, abhorrent, gross,
That on susceptive mould impression clear,
Conspicuous carve; fantastic rites and weird,　　29
That—stablished there—crave vicious permanence.
But thou, choice guide, fleshed by the overthrow
Of passions mutinous—the bearing down
Of rooted prejudice; thou, having once
Ground deftly broke, through stifling of perverse,
Soul-stunting practice (gifts material,
Food—air—allowed the coffined dead, as sane
Provision for their passage to the bourne
Unfading); weaning from inane, deformed
Attachments (reverence for images,
As the depositaries of a force　　40
Whimfully swaying human destinies)
Unquailing, didst on larger strife embark—
To conquest didst more memorable march.

For—converts these as much because coerced
By the strong magnet of thy swerveless walk ;
Fair prizes of thy perfumed probity
(Unwitting incense that the barriered sense,
Assailing, subtly penetrates) as they
Are fruitage of thy brave and fervid toil—
Starved, darkened, blemished, ailing, empty breasts
Found nourished, filled ; illumined, purified.   51

  Rev. J. S.   Little had I accomplished, worthy
Without thine ever-present sympathy ;   [Brant,
Written full oft in active, powerful,
And wise support.   Nor may I disregard
The ready and the useful lever ; nor
Deny th' invaluable impetus
Thy well-deserved, commanding influence
With high and low within thy "Castles'" pale
Unceasing lent.

  Thay.   Repaid my service is,   60
Scanning the lustrous record of thy work.

  Rev. J. S.   Not causelessly elate with what is past—
Gladdened by that review—let us forbear
Urned Retrospection's so capacious mere
For its sunk freight—for its spilled jettison—
O'er mindfully to drag.   Whilst tenderly
Enshrining the closed page, resolve we now
T' augment our stolen success ; the outworks won—

Storm we the muniments. Chasing such end,
Might we not appetize the healthsome food—  70
Of its partakers the soul-teguments—
Bruised, broken, festering—endow, as 'twere
With healing unguent; Great-Heart, might we not
On the glad message saving virtue pour—
Them clothing in the native dialect?

THAY. Such treatment as you signify, dear friend,
The offering would with suasive charm invest;
To it impart a grateful excellence. [schooling; your

REV. J. S. Well, then, your thorough English
Wide cognizance of Mohawk idioms—  80
Fruit from your calling as interpreter
Of Bible story—such equipment would—
If but your aspirations coincide,
Your secret feelings nudge you to assent
To the proposal—wondrously me help
To the fruition of a cherished scheme,
Translation of the Gospel narratives.

THAY. Most heartily I pledge—shall eager bring—
Assistance to that lofty enterprise.
As trowel use my qualities, my gifts,  90
In building that imposing pyramid;
Make requisition on me for the wick
Which should that candle for the nighted grace.
Sweet privilege for both to vindicate,

By dint of free-will measures to extend
The circle of our Church's followers ;
Till there be no left no wanderers to reclaim—
Till there be no left no piners to console ;
All who were hungry have been banqueted—
All who were thirsty have been vivified ;           100
Till there remain no platters to be scoured—
No caverns for Christ-rays to penetrate,
The outflow of that Queenly courtesy ;
Which, toward the birth-hour of the century,
With dower of twin argent services,
Stooped kindly to enrich our altar-stand.
                                         [*Exeunt.*

---

SCENE 2.—PLACE: *The Mohawk Valley—Council-Room at Johnson Hall.*

TIME : *July, 1772.*

GOVERNOR TRYON discovered seated on a raised platform, SIR WM. JOHNSON, by invitation, filling a place at his side ; a number of Indian warriors and women occupying benches in the body of the room. THAYENDANEGEA, coming forward from amongst the male element, addresses the Governor.

THAY.  Come I before you, Sire, as deputy
Of our much-injured Mohawks, to submit
Their case (the controversy represents

The simmering of half a century) 110
Pour in your Excellency's benign ear
Chapter of wrongdoing, by all adjudged
A crying grievance; trouble this which steals
All pleasure from the chase—provides, at night,
The uninviting fabric of our dreams;
A not to be unsaddled incubus.
Relate the linked occurrences to our
Tribe's footing as a land proprietor.
Without assent—nay—even privity,
Of leaguèd sachems, a formality 120
Required to legalize a transfer; plied
With drink the sellers previously had been
(A doltish, irresponsible quintette)
By one George Klock, an odious go-between,
Tracts near Canajoharie—long time dubbed
"The Planting-Grounds," in common parlance—were
Obtained from us by Philip Livingston.
Collins, a land surveyor, presently—
To aggravate our hardship—undertook
T' increase the boundaries materially; 130
Achievement—to evade our vigilance—
Compassed by stealth, upon a moonlight tour;
Claiming the ampler premises to be
Th' original dimensions of the grant.
The Congress, afterwards (let me say here

The complot in its full enormity
Was not revealed for nearly twenty years)
Asked to explore that cave of guilt—inspect
That slough of turpitude—reported that
The maudlin transferors no status had           140
Th' estate to alienate.   Accepted this
By chief successor of the patentee;
But there being infant heirs, not competent
To voice their wish, things hung in abeyance;
Till German settlers 'gan to squat upon
The questioned lands.   Our "Castles," here, to gain
Due recognition as their overlords,
Collection pressed from these of stated rent—
In money this long paid, or money's worth.
The younger Livingston, to complicate           150
Affairs, tried to eject our husbandmen;
While Klock—the sneaking mongrel at his heels—
Exceeding loath to disappoint the hopes
Formed from his facile graduation as
A scoundrel; fresh-assailing, with a more
Unstinted use of liquor, new-found dupes,
Prevailed upon them to relinquish rights,
By all possessed, in common, in the block;
Admitting thus the sale's validity:
Wringing, besides, confirmatory deed            160
Unto himself and fit associate.

Later, to do him justice, Livingston—
When were elicited the naked facts,
Fully exposed the glaring roguery—
Before a Council specially convened,
A proper willingness displayed to bow
To its unfavorable arbitrament;
But Klock, who had acquired part ownership,
Flatly refuses to undo his fraud.
Wherefore, we trust your Excellency's power    170
Will be exerted to recover that,
Which your mild predecessor, Monckton, held
To 've been most shamefully, most wickedly,
Purloined; that you'll be swift to imprecate
Torrential evil on that guileful class
Of pale-face ruffians (of whom this Klock's
The loathsome archetype) who trap—delude;
Contaminate—corrupt; that levelled may
Be jaggèd slugs of obloquy at those
(Klock most malodorous of the harpy spawn,    180
None of the genus so insatiate)
Whose unclean, lawless trade it is to steep
Too yielding brains in brandy's poisonous fumes,
To serve their foul, their sordid interest.
Not populous are we; nor—singly—boast
We noted strength. Still have we frequent proved
That we can manage proud connections; we,

Seeking, can rivet firm alliances:
So we believe you'll impulse find to turn
To the redressing of our grievances, 190
In the great danger of its going abroad;
Should you betray a mocking negligence—
Take refuge in a listless apathy—
That safeguards we from Britain's crown derived
Had been by you disparaged—disesteemed;
That aught had chanced to weaken, or to dull
The covenant-chain our sires redoubtable
Have long preserved intact—leave luminous;
That items of our nation's privilege
Were trampled—scouted; ridiculed—ignored. 200

 Gov. Tryon. Stout orator, your warm recital, if
In no wise strained, or colored, must awake
Responsive thrill in every righteous breast;
Therefore, you may depend upon it that
My utmost—everything—I'll do to bring
About the restitution of your rights.
       [*Exeunt omnes.*

SCENE 3.—PLACE: *The Mohawk Valley—Lawn at Johnson Hall, the Manor-House of the Superintendent of Indian Affairs.*

TIME: *Midsummer, 1773.*

*Enter* THAYENDANEGEA *and* SIR WILLIAM JOHNSON.

SIR WM. JOHNSON. Supplies for me, good Joseph,
Of joysome meditation that in this [constant theme
Tossed undersphere my usual goings have
Been so disposed that Providence permits          210
Me pleasured eye, at will, to throw o'er these
Bright confines—landscape that of beauty, charm,
Uncovers infinite diversity.
While from these banked parterres the thrallèd ken
Broad tilth surveys, which, slanting towards the town,
Abuts like surface bending hitherward;
The field of vision equally gives room
For compact area of tranquil plain:
Far off, those sun-bathed, lucent levels seen
Merging in rampired slope; channèlled or else   220
By peaceful vale. Partitioned wondrously,
That restful floor (a map spread of unflawed
Tessellar paving, or seeming of some
Ideal patchwork, they, the dainty and
The trim resultant) into polished strips

Of fructed glebe; with pleasant, emerald-
Hued zones of thrifty pasture, here and there
Them bordering; effulgent quarterings—
Their essence printed on each spearlet's soft,
As comely head-dress—which, with vividness,   230
Attest the free, the buoyant stimulus
Of careful tillage—cheerfully reflect
Th' incentive stroke of flagless industry.
Sheds this kind region choicest specimen
Of air-dosed cereal—earth-bowed vegetal;
Of fruit of vine each mellow variant—
All sweets of groaning orchard best affords:
Return produced, at times, should but the door
Unlatched be of a bursting treasure-house.
The scene holds other prospect; Nature there   240
Doffing her robe of sumptuous elegance,
But to reveal as grateful spectacle—
Stretches of wind-stirred uplands. Yonder sprawl
The Mayfield Hills, tree-turbaned; southward rise
(Cloud-piercing minarets) through wreathing haze,
The peaks of Cherry Valley. Nor deprived
The chequered view of grandeur's complement—
Transepts of cloistral forest. Struck, perchance—
So viewing it—the note of rhapsody;
Yet would I estimate this cirque terrene,   250
Where jostle lea and cope arboreal;

Mate humid dales with lonely, spectral hills,
Grass-quilted croft with herb-sprent table-land—
Marvel of the Creator's handiwork.

 THAYENDANEGEA.   Nowise too partial verdict;
The rapture such oped vista in my breast   [emulous
Enkindles—sating picture which sustains
With famed Schoharie pushing rivalry.

 SIR WM. J.   Faithful disciple, instant to defend
Your habitation as the King; whose cause—    260
Ramified empire—strengthened were through your
Suppression of the Delawares; support
Towards humbling headstrong Pontiac, as well
As at your fiery christening. Tell truth,
The borrowed sway—that easy, light-held rein
Laid on the haunch of your communities—
At urgent wish of Brunswick's honored House
On me devolved; a tempered tutelage;
Surveillance, which has served, in thin disguise
Of teasing curb, the lures to counteract    270
Of sly self-seekers (with the seemly show
Of state annexed to its bland exercise)
Could not, through trying span of troubled years,
Have been by me administered in just
Degree; maintained in full security,
Had not your boundless, your unfaltering trust—
Your steadfast and your pure devotion—stood

Tall bulwark of my person and my place—
Firm holdfast for a way-worn voyager.  279
 Thay. An ingrate I, had I done otherwise!
Who planned to train my mind's crude faculties?
Who showers upon me worldly benefits?
The wine decants of public rectitude?
Ah! generous patron, golden counsellor,
Work—deeds—of mine can never these requite.
 Sir Wm. J. Treating of your domestic happenings—
You late a close-matched fencing tourney waged,
I hear, with your celestial guide—the topic sprung
Your second marriage. With what wardless lunge
Sought you to stab the rigorous tenet: weds  290
No man the sister of departed wife?
 Thay. Such unions I upheld, as I contend,
By valid logic—theory that one
Already a blood-relative would love
More tenderly her offspring who had died,
Than one confessing no affinity. [to convince?
 Sir Wm. J. You failed, though, austere Stuart
 Thay. Despite my pressing the contention that
The wisdom of our tribes endorsed these pacts.
Since my rebuff, a German Lutheran  300
Divine, whose teaching showed more latitude—
Dared to disown strait-laced theologies—
Conceded us the boon solicited.

Sir Wm. J.  How prospers, by the way, the task
Stuart and you proceed in unison ?   [with which
You know I feel a special interest
In any such commendable attempts :
No spurring needed to co-operate
With Colonel Claus, my elder son-in-law ;
Who managed, with much patience, to convert   310
Into your Canienga the chaste text
Of our surpassless Book of Common Prayer ;
Lending the while every encouragement
In perfecting his helpful alphabet.
    Thay.  St. Mark's account has been construed ;
      the Acts
Of the Apostles now engages us.
    Sir Wm. J.  The page will be a during monument ;
It to your glory, credit must redound—
Production worthy, which, I'm satisfied,
Will long endear you to posterity.   320
                              [*Exeunt.*

SCENE 4.—PLACE: *Interior of the same.*

TIME: *Christmas, 1773.*

*Enter* SIR WILLIAM JOHNSON *and* MAJOR JOHN BUTLER, *who converse together before a window which commands an unobstructed view of the grounds in front.*

MAJOR BUTLER.  Please you it must, Sir William,
   to observe
The growth—prosperity—of Johnstown; how
About a slender nucleus has formed
The dignified, brisk centre of a shire.

SIR WM. JOHNSON.  Yes; it has been a child of
   much strong-felt
Affection.

MAJOR BUTLER.  You'll not fail to recollect
How cordially the Governor approved
Its model order; large contentedness.

(COLONEL GUY JOHNSON *is here seen approaching, with agitation traceable in looks and mien.*)

SIR WM. J.  Why hurries Guy this way?  His
A tale of gravest import.                [face prefers

(*To Guy Johnson.*)   Guy, what makes   330
Your countenance the seat of care—reflex
Of wan anxiety.
  GUY JOHNSON.  Sirs, I have just
Returned from Boston; where still walks abroad—
Asserts itself through stir assiduous,
With gall implacable—that bugbear fell,
The Tea-tax.  Lived again those moments when
Choked was in tumult, wrath, its congener,
The Stamp Act: then the rabble, need I tell,
'Mid other proofs of a fanatic craze,
Sacked the Chief Justice' sightly residence;   340
And—gloating—hung in effigy the Stamp-
Provider.  Seethings, rumblings, mutterings—
Scared mortals treading o'er an Ætna's crust;
Commotion—uproar—reigning in all streets;
A very carnival of terrorism.
Fluent aspersings of the Monarchy;
Treason, in very truth, hawked everywhere—
Labelled untainted, licit merchandise.
Gathered upon the wharves I saw a rash—
A fevered—group (whose two-score ringleaders   350
Paraded there as buck-skinned savages)
Minded to rush to criminal extreme;
Should the officials at the port attempt
To board the fleet of bending merchantmen,

Then entering the harbor with their freight,
To force the loathèd impost.   This the pale,
Uneasy placemen—duteous, if not
Discreet—with dull reluctance set about
To do ; the "braves," nimbly forestalling them,
Vaulted the gunwales ; with alacrity,            360
Staving the chests which their distemper stirred,
Plunged their contents with fury in the brine.
   Sir Wm. J.   Patent to me that fresh vitality
Was made to animate Sedition's breast
By Franklin's greetings.   He translated for
Its bustling fold sense of the multitude
In England that their braving policy's
Continuance would melt the Parliament ;
Sending therewith (the missives neatly bagged
By a recourse to shady artifice)                 370
Scripts of the Massachusetts Governor—
Of Oliver, his able adjutant—
Penned months before being trickishly unearthed,
(All but two mild ones of the series
When not yet seated in their offices)
To correspondent on the Commons-Roll ;
Coupled with strictures on Bostoniáns,
Roughly arraigning the Assembly's work ;
Which pressed—its anger sluiced —for their recall ;
Request we may, with confidence, assume          380

The Ministry with curtness will rebuke—
Chilling-asperity—refuse outright.

    MAJOR BUTLER. Well, I, for one, feel greatly
By the reflection that disorder thrives   [comforted
Uncertainly in this eloignèd vale.

        [*Exeunt* GUY JOHNSON *and* MAJOR BUTLER.

    SIR WILLIAM JOHNSON (*solus*).
How I do shrink from the decision, which
Will, soon or late, infallibly be thrust
Upon me by these gloomy visitants—
Precursors gruff of my climacteric!
What chance to lessen the disturbances—     390
What prospect to survive in quietude
Th' exaggerated tension—of the times?
Whose form but dangles o'er a precipice;
Or sees above the sword of Damocles?
Reduced are all in common here to suck
The bale-fraught vapors of the atmosphere.
Nor could I—were my havior optional—
Be satisfied to hedge; in such ill day
Consent to temporize. Find I myself
Blest with enjoyment of rare affluence;     400
To station lifted of distinction—weight—
Of much consideration in the land,
By virtue of the State's munificence.

The " Royal Grant "—douceur conferred of near
Seventy thousand acres far outstretched
(The broadest messuage in the colony)
Commuted fairly though the bounty was
For zeal intense, life-long activity :
These, with the dignity of baronet ;
My son's endowing with the accolade—  410
Could I put off less dunning creditors,
Quiet the beggar of formed preferences ;
Apart from the persuasion that my past
With such endeavor's easiest to be squared,
Plead with me to maintain the dynasty.
Impressed am I, nathless, by some of those
Abuses that the recusants advance
For disaffection : crusty Governors—
Highly imbued with alien sympathies ;
The truncheon waving of intolerance ;  420
Measures conceived—to parturition brought—
Without the people's sanction ; others quite
As rudely thwarted which they advocate :
Vicious o'erstepping of prerogatives.
These levies—birth short-sighted, mischievous,
Laid in defiance of entreaty—claimed,
Despite expostulations lodged by those
On whom they press ; rule rigid which ordains
Trans-ocean carriage of commodities

In British hulls : full grating fiats—some     430
E'en flavored with nutmeg Draconian.
Howe'er the merits of the sides compare,
Peril must I—when longer none shall be
Buoyed by illusion, lulled to somnolence—
The life of a full-podded stalk ; when it
Incumbent is to cross *my* Rubicon,
Hazard do I wealth, regal revenues—
All my possessions in a lottery ;
I—when I am compelled to cast the die—
Gamble with power, dominion, influence ;     440
Hypothecate a priceless property.

                     [*Exit* SIR WILLIAM JOHNSON.

SCENE 5.—PLACE: *The Mohawk Valley—A public place in Johnstown.*

TIME: *June, 1774.*

*Enter* THAYENDANEGEA *and* MAJOR JOHN BUTLER.

THAYANDANEGEA. Ah! Butler, I have lost my
Most gracious benefactor!         [truest friend—
  MAJOR BUTLER.         Mean you, Brant,
Noble Sir William ?
  THAY.         None, alas, but he.    [account.
  MAJOR B. Distressful news ! Give me the full
  THAY. He had been ill; but his wide tact—his
Invited to allay a tempest raised         [skill—
Amongst our sensitive confederacy,
By murders wrought by some Virginians
Of members of two Pennsylvania tribes—         450
Heads of the Delawares, the Shawanese;
Kindred of Logan, the Cayuga (who
Labored the coalition to involve
In plot to fall upon the border, as
Reprisal for this " Cresap " massacre)
Duty outvoting prudence ; instantly
Misgivings quelled—the invalid sunk in

The pacifier—left his couch to hold
A Council. At the Sittings—long drawn out—
He taxed his strength in an exhaustive speech. 460
This led to irremediable relapse
Of his complaint.
    MAJOR BUTLER. Bound to be violent
Upflaring from that spark; match lit that fired
The magazine! The panic set afoot,
In fact, developed such intensity—
Mounted so quickly to high-water mark—
Your synod had convened before my aid,
Due as their regular interpreter,
Could be bespoken to convey the gist
Of the debates.
    THAY. With such wild eagerness 470
Rushed the grim huntsman to annihilate
The stricken quarry, that Sir John; housed then
In former mansion of the baronet—
Fort Johnson—distant, as you know, but nine
Quick-traversable miles from thence; albe
Of his condition swift-apprized; and though,
In essay his fleet rival to outstrip,
Excelling speed of dust-ringed chariot
In ancient games Olympian (his horse,
Succumbing to the strain, dropped dead beneath 480
His rider, forcing him to beg a friend's)

Entered the patient's room only to find
The once discerning sense in rouseless state
Of coma plunged.

    Major Butler. There, chieftain, was withdrawn
A beacon-light for unsure mariners!
Plain finger-post for pilgrim's reference!
His every talent serving to exalt—
All added graces fitted to adorn—
A public character; a stature reached
By no contemporary. In statesmanship     490
(For one with attributes so masterful,
Too narrow, too obscure the theatre)
Who was with that adept heard to contest
The primacy: as guarded as astute
In broad negotiations with the tribes—
Exerting in this field a subtle art
Withal, a magic potency (digest
Th' immortal treaty with the Senecas;
The fused bands at Stanwix) think how sued
To him for pardon lordly Pontiac.     500
Winning, in youth, through native manfulness,
Each tilt with Fortune; for brain-capital
Expended in all walks indemnity.
Of War, to our joyed vision, testified
He knowledge, like to Clive's, intuitive
(Witness Lake George and Fort Niagara).

A service of his King, which hazard recked
Not—a devotion toil intensified.
Commerce—consider the vast profits reaped
From early barterings.  Holding aloft 510
The torch of honor and of probity
In all relations; wasteful of his time—
Means—energy, whene'er the general good
Required them : loosing, at command, a flood
Of glowing, of persuasive eloquence ;
(His lucid play of feature advertised
The volant envoy from the inner self,
Trustworthy dial, on whose tell-tale face
Was read the shifting meter of the soul)
Focus of social courtesies ; renowned 520
His wealth of flowing hospitality.
A temper genial—a deportment suave ;
Consistent, mild humanitarian.
A churchmanship despising bigotry ;
As proof hereof stood out his readiness
(The fragrance from the vased bloom still regales)
His purse to open to assist the plans—
The hands to strengthen, and the progress aid—
Further the interests of every sect.

THAY.  Yet dissidents amongst the townspeople
The rancorous supposition forthwith coined 531
That he himself—faced by th' impending schism,—

The flame of life had impiously quenched;
Judgment they clinch with screws of circumstance:
Clue hailed as best index of verity,
The saying, in chance conversation passed
With a familiar, that he would not be
Alive to see the Provinces in arms;
Dash further of the sauce of likelihood
To add—that on the day of his decease            540
His lineaments had mirrored singular
Emotion, packet conning he was then
Observed to open from the Minister;
Requesting action, which would from him have
Wrested avowal of his sentiments.
Yet seemed his end entirely natural;
For at the Hall my sister read me note,
Which his physician sent with medicine;
In which collapse was pointedly foretold,
Should strong excitement—bodily fatigue—         550
Be undergone. The casual speech which he
Let fall vague premonition of his near
Demise merely expressed, which prompted was
By course of his progressive malady.
Besides, in April last (indulging vein
Here, too, of melancholy prophecy)
He, writing to the Earl of Dartmouth, had
Supported prayer that his then deputy,

Guy Johnson, should succeed him in his post,
By statement that his health, at best, was most   560
Precarious; the train of physical
Infirmities his unrelaxed employ—
Civil and military—had induced
Him warning that his early death was all
Too probable.
    MAJOR BUTLER.   Oppressed though you may be,
Old friend—with him in closest contact brought—
With sense of loss more personal than ours;
Of one, who, by consent, will occupy
Distinguished niche in Fame's high Pantheon;
To whom the living shall a place assign   570
Red-lettered in Remembrance' calendar;
Whose kindly actions—output of a mine
Well-nigh exhaustless—will (howbeit for good
The carnal tent's unstaked) culled ingots, shine,
Coruscant in Affection's treasury;
Whose spendthrift generosity—which so
Impartial showed itself as oftentimes
To comprehend, in its vast plenitude,
His country's enemies—spontaneous
Tribute evoked from its recipients,   580
In presence of this sore bereavement, which
Makes poor as well the nation as the King,
The countryside a common sorrow feels.
                                         [*Exeunt.*

SCENE 6.—PLACE: *The Mohawk Valley—Farm of*
JOHN VEEDER, *near Caughnawaga.*

TIME: *May, 1775.*

A knot of revolutionists—a larger gathering surrounding them—among whom are the owner of the farm and SAMPSON SAMMONS, are preparing to erect a "Liberty Pole."

SAMPSON SAMMONS (*to John Veeder*).   Be it our
   office, Herr, to imitate
Boston's high spirit ; which has suitably—
Emblem adopting such as we propose—
Marked its profound abhorrence of this gross,
Unending tyranny ;  too long in mean
Subjection held, blazed its intent to slip
The yoke of servitude.

   JOHN VEEDER.   Aim I commend.            590
      (*Turning to the crowd.*)
Good people ; who by solemn vow are pledged
To beard—subdue—the despot ; end your term
As cumbered pack-mules, sweating galley-slaves ;
Like Israel under Pharaoh's dominance,
Galled drudges of an iron taskmaster,
By deeds make good your plighted word ; confirm
Your resolution ; climb the steeps ahead ;

Your palms pressing the plough, look not behind.
Leaks plugging in your courage, lend a hand
To rear our rustic " Pole of Liberty."         600
So seize we glove flung by the Sessions ; so
Frame we reply to truckling Magistrates !

(*They are still busied with the work, when they are
interrupted by the arrival of two or three hundred
armed retainers of* SIR JOHN JOHNSON; *at whose head
are the baronet,* COLONELS DANIEL CLAUS *and* GUY
JOHNSON, *and* MAJOR BUTLER. COLONEL GUY JOHNSON,
*mounting the stoop of the Caughnawaga Church — a
property adjoining the* VEEDER *farm—proceeds to harangue the assemblage.*)

 GUY JOHNSON. What harvest think to glean,
  misguided throng,
From seed now sown of rank disloyalty?
Though Massachusetts claim the right to base,
On pressure of extreme enactments, plea
For flying in the face of Government;
Leaving Virginia to nurse her spite—
Lend pleased asylum to the canker-worm ;
Dwells there meet pretext for Disunion's snarl     610
(Bad upshot of your shaky sophistries—)
In tenor of events transpiring *here* ?
*Your* trade is not deranged—not sealed *your* ports ;

Quartered on *you* no regulative troops;
Wounds bringing smart to a community,
Which merits well the King's displeasure. Have
Your charters been revoked; impends o'er *you*
That lash invented for recalcitrants—
Citation harsh to Westminster for crimes?
Reckless, purblind incendiaries, take thought!   620
Strife-fanners—were a rupture justified—
What genuine assurance of success,
In guilty call to arms to realize
Your pestilent theories, poor fools; which this
Opening the floodgates of your turbulence;
Hasty unbottling of an ogreish force
(The Fisherman freeing the Genie)
Directly instigates, can you embrace?
Forms the lean episode of Lexington—
That feeble splutter of the minute-men—   630
The bolster for your gospel of disdain?
Has our age-owned supremacy become
So slight a thing—so shaken, tottering—
That Albion's stewards overseas could not
Cohorts enough control to crush your mad
Revolt? Your beggarly militia—they
With Britain's seasoned veterans contend!
A single ship of her proud navy—roar
From its death-spewing fissures—could prevent

All useful operations on the main.  640
Laced are the trade-ways by a string of forts.
Enlist we shall, with ease, upon our side
The border Indians; though th' Oneidas have,
By leaving us untimely in the lurch,
Their record sullied; still the Mohawks and
The Senecas, the Onondagas and
Cayugas (Tuscaroras, mayhap,) we
Can summon to our aid if we're attacked.
Abandon, then ('twill much conduce to your  649
Own weal) your wilful work—yourselves correct
Its spirit of affront; arrest, while time
Befriends, the gangrene of contumacy;
Engaol the hydra-felon—lawlessness.
Else, hot-heads, look for some gust-brewing Thor
*That* Jötun of confusion to afflict—
For some avenging Michael, rage-possessed,
*That* Belial of defection to o'erthrow.

SAMPSON SAMMONS. Desist, thou supple tool of
State-coddled parcel of subservience,      [Royalty;
Dam up your sultry pratings! What about  660
This irksome tribute, that the Parliament
Grimly exacts; high-handed vetoings
Imposed on commerce with each foreign mart;
Joined to the British merchants' noxious grant
Of a monopoly of gainful trades—

The fossil ordinance by which we've been
Barred income from the coastwise fisheries ;
Used all to render stagnant Traffic's stream ;
On Progress' vessel stuck like barnacles :
The mode ta'en th' independence to crush out— 670
The fairness—of the Judges, by the Crown's
Lifting the spoon that buys servility :
A dogma-harnessed King—with Governors ;
Who, to promote their usurpations ; who,
In preaching of their brusque evangel, and
In pushing of their strained pretensions, would
Tread down—intimidate—our councillors.
Why gendered wonder—why professed surprise—
When manly, free-born subjects ; staggering
With burdens under which they groan—hewers 680
Of wood, drawers of water—ills resist ;
Which Life have made a breachèd citadel ;
Contentment a crestfallen fugitive ;
Pleasure a phantom ; Peace a travesty ;
Which thrust them in a pit of misery ;
Which hack them with the knife of cruelty :
Marooning them on Island of Despair,
Would every hopeful prospect sepulchre ;
Each reasonable yearning immolate.
How you misjudge our weakness—magnify 690
Your strength ; unmoved, presuming oracle,

We list your forecast of our impotence;
Await the season of our chastisement—
The promised crashing of the thunderbolt—
With sinews braced.  Vain braggart, were you not
Enthroned their overseer, your crooked power
Over those blind, unthinking savages,
On whose co-operation you rely,
Count would but as the veriest feather-weight.   699

    Guy Johnson.   Arch-breeder—nourisher—of dis-
Disgusting and how coarse your animus! [cord, how
With what unconscionable acrimony
Have you traduced the nation's law-givers;
With what unwearied, blatant vehemence
Have you contemned the King's authority!

    Sampson Sammons.  I would not be the throne-
        propped minion—
Lower myself to play the sycophant—
I see before me for the pilèd wealth
Of this fair pleasaunce.

    Guy Johnson.           Vaporous malcontent!
You and your gang of rioters give heed.            710
Half-wakened Loyalty could want no ruder pinch;
Long-suffering, pocket no grosser wrong.
She—thus beset, thus hounded—feels constrained
The muzzle of prevention to apply
To Insubordination—clap upon

Sedition's wrists the handcuffs of restraint;
Her interdict 'gainst reinless license turns,
At last, to promulgate: maddened, insists
On yonder eyesore being at once laid low—
On shivering of that vile "rock of offence."        720
Your personal innuendoes, calumnies
I pass in scornful silence—choose to treat
As flaws from the abominable reek
Bred in a pest-house of malignity.

*Mutually inflamed, the recriminators rush upon each other, and are only torn apart after a furious struggle.* SAMMONS *is soon after struck down by a riding-whip in the hands of* COLONEL GUY JOHNSON'S *equerry. Recovering from the blow, he rises to his feet; and, discarding his coat, prepares to renew the fight. He is, however, beaten down a second time by a couple of strokes from some King's-man's bludgeon. Rising again, he finds that his sympathizers have all decamped. At this point, the Royalists, having first wrenched from its place, and levelled to the earth, the repulsive emblem, also draw off.*

END OF ACT II.

# ACT III.

SCENE 1.—PLACE: *The Mohawk Valley—Guy Park, residence of* COLONEL GUY JOHNSON.

TIME: *May, 1775.*

*Enter* THAYENDANEGEA, SIR JOHN JOHNSON *and* COLONEL GUY JOHNSON.

SIR JOHN JOHNSON. These amateur rebuilders—
saviours wise—
Of our rent Commonwealth seem exercised
About my attitude. I've cause to know
That they dislike those brawny Highlanders
(Macdonells with no paltry pedigree)
The bulk distributed on my estates,
Near Caughnawaga, and about Tribes Hill;
A stalwart brood of native soldiery;
Which—new-imported from the parent soil—
They truly deem unshaken Royalists;          10
Looking askance, as well—with grave mistrust—
At steps we're taking now to fortify
Our manors.

Guy Johnson. As for me, great need to be
Prepared; for I've been told, through messages
From trusty brethren, that some viperous
New Englanders propose to seize me; I
Keep at my beck, in consequence, a squad
To fend me were some ill turn to befall.

Sir John J. I'll wage remembrance of our resolute
Protection of the sheriff; whom they chose  20
To view bedaubed with pitch of Erebus,
Rankles in depths of their degenerate breasts.

Thayendanegea (*to Guy Johnson*). Bending the
   survey to *our* household's state—
You, doubtless, lively pleasure have derived
From knowledge that the unmatched usefulness—
Outspoken ardor—of yourself and Frey,
As stable buttresses of Monarchy,
Lent from this district to the Council: that
Your zeal—combativeness (prompt to lock horns
With sinewed gladiators) these have been  30
Applauded by the Supervisors.

Guy Johnson.                    Yes;
Their action was as staunch as opportune.
Still—though they emphasized the doctrine sound,
That nothing reckoned indispensable
To living was affected by the tax;
Nor general trade, through its exaction, hurt,

The Tryon Magistracy's—Sessions'—views
Cropped out in most explicit verbiage:
"Spurn we the thought of other partnerships;
We cannot tolerate time-servers; we     40
Scorn to descend to phrase equivocal,
Slipping from tongues of spineless waverers."
The Council, furthermore, have negatived
A motion made to thank the delegates
To the initial Congress; while they froze
Another to appoint fresh Amorites.
I might remark, here, incidentally,
That I have cautioned Kirkland; who the nod
Accepts from Boston's offal, to refrain
From stirring up (his will, you know, with them
Is paramount) th' Oneidas 'gainst the King.     51
Petitioned by the Bund to mediate
With flexile boughs of the confederacy,
One willing function he discharges now—
Judged this to be by Massachusetts Bay
Malignants a proceeding politic—
Is conduit for transmitting to his charge
Of Indians the Congress' doings, met
At Philadelphia. Friends, recognize
In him we must a shrewd antagonist;     60
Having already the Oneidas pledged
To the adoption of a neutral stand:

Though I much fear they'll yet decide to grasp
The hatchet for the insurrectionists.

   Sir John J.  The impudent contrivance to allure,
By counsel tendered through the Mohicans,
The purer factors of that notable
Amalgam to the separatists' camp,
I'm pleased to learn, though, has been profitless.
Mention of Kirkland, by the by, reminds      70
Of Joseph's rather crabbed aphorism;
(The quip have I permission to retail?)
When stumbling on an apple, none too ripe:
" As sour as any Congregational."

   Thay.  The ill-luck that befell the carrier
Of the remonstrance sounded by our chiefs
To those defaulters; wherein I, the scribe,
Ventured to chide them for their dalliance
With phase of your kidnapping, Colonel Guy—
Unseasonable loss of the despatch,      80
After prehension by unfriendly hand—
That two-pronged misadventure, no doubt, brought
Kirkland a whetstone whereupon to edge
His skill to nullify our influence.
I late received a letter from my good
Old teacher, Doctor Wheelock; in it he
Invited me to back the Colonists.
I winged him blunt retort; saying I could

Not disobey his grand injunction pressed:
"While serving God, through each mutation shaped,
To honor steadfastly—whole-heartedly—  91
The King; always contented subjects live."

  SIR JOHN J.  Rejoinder, truly, most appropriate;
Rock-builded purpose travelled in its strain!

(*A large concourse of Indians is noticed entering the park enclosure.*)

  GUY JOHNSON.  My Mohawks come, bid to a
    colloquy!

(*The Indians, having ranged themselves conveniently around him, are now addressed by their Superintendent.*)

True-hearted tribesmen! I have little fear
That you'll not stay us in extremity;
Still, would I, warriors, have you ponder facts,
Which, clarion-lunged, ask your fidelity:
The foremost—England's magnanimity;  100
Her upright, honest treatment of your race
For cycle that o'erruns a century;
The furnishing of forts to stem the French
Incursions.  Safety gave she to your trade;
When guilds among the Dutch, at Albany—
Intriguing openly to cross you—would
Fain have admitted the destructionist.

And did they not—grafts from that pelf-grained
Having, with promise of fair-dealing, once   [stock—
Bargained with you for highly-favored slice         110
Of your domains—productive champaign near
Shenectady—with peerless hardihood,
O'erlook the crucial incident of pay ?
Where found to-day that grasping company ?
Do they not herd with the Provincials : pant
Afflictive—even mortal—blow to deal
At British influence ; intruded oft
As an impervious barricade to shield
You ; pitted ever warmly, avidly,
Against their devious conspiracies ?                  120
Braves, mindful of that unblest interval ;
Break when Warraghiyagey did resign
The seals of office to Commissioners
(A venal board, not answerable save
To partial Junta of the colony)
Espy you not a just criterion—
Should the insurgents (Heaven forfend) succeed,
In selfishness—innate uncharity—
Of churls (who, ledger-married, scout the " Live
And let live "—ban the civil ethics such            130
Terse sermon recommends) by which to judge
Their wild, disruptive faction's future acts ?
Are you not certain to be flouted—ay—

Elbowed aside ? Wreaking on you a spleen
Retributive, all debts will they not squeeze
With usury ? Be wise, then, in your day
And generation ! Load the scale with us !
Your prowess, so expended, must preclude
Arrival of such dread catastrophe :
Mohawks, abstain from mixing for yourselves 140
Ingredients of a cup of bitterness !
Pause, Mohawks, ere assuring for yourselves
A dismal epoch of adversity !

    CANASTOTA. Have thou, our apt, high-minded mentor, no
Concern for us ; warm-nested memories
Of favors done us by Sir William—thought
Of his ungrudging care, kind guardianship ;
Of his disinterested benevolence ;
Even were motives far less capital
Adduced than those, by which you urgently 150
Exhort us at this juncture ominous
T' approve our stand as Britain's liegemen, would
*Alone* suffice to fix our constancy ;
With hooks us fasten to his family.
                        [*Exeunt omnes.*

SCENE 2.—Place: *Montreal—Executive-Mansion.*

*Enter* Thayendanegea, Sir Guy Carleton *and*
Colonel Guy Johnson.

   Sir Guy Carleton. Colonel, I understand that
      you and Brant—
Tried standby of the House of Hanover;
Whose compact sworn with ancient Albion
Has been kept strictly—held inviolate;
Whom we must thank for having volunteered
To lend his nation as material                160
To caulk the seams in our adventurous—
In our gale-braving, our high-riding bark:
As solder to repair the crevices,
Which Time, the licensed tamperer—unseen,
Insidious erosive; noiseless, yet
Unresting frayer—rude disintegrant
In the utensil must create, intend
To visit in the fall the Mother-land.
   Col. Guy Johnson. Yes, there is much to lay
      before the throne;
Chief point—the wisdom and propriety       170
Of an employment of the Indians.
   Sir Guy C. Use the occasion, prithee, to impart
True inwardness of the embroglio;

Advise whose are the hands that intermix
The livening yeast with that intestine dough.
   (*To Thay.*) As to a union with the savages—
Brant, think you you can check their fieriness;
Coax some accession to their ballasting?
You know my feeling; that I deprecate
A general service of these adjuvants;      180
Believing that it should be limited
To work of scouts, of guides and couriers;
Quick-scented beagles to beat up the game.
   THAYENDANEGEA. Your Excellency may rest
That, subjected to prudent oversight      [satisfied
(And such shall not be wanting, I engage,)
They will not prove themselves refractory;
Will neither cut the cords of discipline;
Nor deviate from the grooves of steadiness.
Our course, Sire, should moreover, I submit,    190
Be regulated by the enemy's:
Who—furbished up their stock appliances—
Their gullets tempt with every sort of bait;
Their nostrils titillate with odorous musk;
Their ears besiege with specious oratory:
Approach with presents—offer bonuses—
As taking fillips to lay by the heels
A plethora of fighting Royalists;
Draw herrings numerous across the trail,

In hope of vanquishing the scruples which 200
They feel about deserting their allies.
  Sir Guy C. I trust they may not, chief, fail in
    the test.
Be this, however, as it may, you're sure
Of cordial reception from the King.
  Thay. Kora, the scent of war kindles my blood
Implanted in—nursed by—th' aborigine
A love of Nature, Nature's harmonies.
Thrilled is he by the outlook on the heavens'
Compareless majesty—their stately calm—
Their deep and pure infinitude; takes joy 210
From their resplendent streaking—coloring.
While prizing high those sovereign delights;
Nature's soul-filling, sweet tranquillity;
Uplifted, when intently pondering
The strikingness of her phenomena—
Attracted by the wondrous pageantry,
Hushed in the presence of the mysteries:
Though charmèd, too, by Music's dulcet tones—
The ecstasies it yields, the solacements—
Rich concord, innocent of parallel; 220
Music, with its mystical influence—
Touching appeal, heart-message recondite;
Music with its enjoyment sensuous—
Impassioned flow, vibrating utterance;

The deep-mouthed organ's bold, exultant note—
Sonorous swell; the pedalled harpischord's
Appeasing melody—soft cadences;
More keenly stirred am I—more mightily—
By peal of trumpet, noise of drum; these make
My heart beat quick—each fibre permeate.      230
                              [*Exeunt omnes.*

---

SCENE 3.—PLACE: *Plain adjoining Fort Niagara.*

        TIME: *September, 1776.*

A largely-attended convention of chiefs and warriors of the Six-Nations, Delawares, Chippewas, Wyandots, Pottawatomies, and other tribes found assembled under a spacious marquee; with MAJOR JOHN BUTLER, as Superintendent of Indian Affairs, *pro tem.*, presiding.

MAJOR JOHN BUTLER (*addressing the congress*).
Proud stems of the historic Iroquois;
Chiefs, warriors, from west—from south—
Who with my precept have so willingly
Complied; the arched horizon everywhere
O'ercast—the look-out on all sides such as to breed
Concern—I ask all those comprising this
Impressive gathering to intimate

Their views.  The discontented shoot throws off
The mask ; till last July he brayed pretence
Of warring for a meliorated sway ;  240
With folly since—a childish waywardness—
He's frankly mutinied : has seized the ship ;
Yard-armed the helmsman, and the captain brained ;
Has rudder smashed, and friendly compass spurned.
Weighing pivotal feature of the strife,
How much endurance—pertinacity—
What grade of stamina should be to men,
Think you, attributed, who find themselves
Hunted in half a year from Canada ?
Sequel promoted when we checkmate dealt  250
Vainglorious Allen through his prisonment ;
Sequel assured when they repulse severe
(Six-Nations, you, its leading instruments)
In impact at the "Cedars" (fuming surge,
Which, blending erelong with the placider
"Cascades," reforms its mood ; buries its wrath
In bowl of Lake St. Louis) underwent.
*There* had they never feeblest footing got,
Had not its people lacked stability ;
Lost to all pride, all decency, while swift  260
To demonstrate their flabby loyalty,
Forced us unbar both Chamblée and St. John's :
Cause that for our vacating Montreal.

SANGUERACHTA (*spokesman for the Senecas*).

From porters at the western threshold placed,
Friends—kinsmen—to our time-creased heritage
A cordial welcome, though the storm-cloud lowers;
(Would you were guests at jocund festival;
Were bidden but to smoke the calumet)
To region where; while yet th' indulgent seas
Walled out the white man's wilting avarice,    270
Our fathers coursed, at will, the prairie; or,
Upspringing, faced the wild's fierce tenantry;
When they, the zestful chase' sole devotees,
The bow-string curved—the cleaving paddle flashed;
New-comers none them seeking to supplant.
Age *that* of lustre—dignity—which oft,
Detained in fancy's mesh, I contemplate;
When was the wigwam liberally decked
With moving trophies—garniture—of war;
When bred was stock of mould inflexible—    280
Strangers to aught less than pre-eminence,
Each one an independent emperor—
Souls that dictation brooked, supremacy
Allowed of none. Existence halcyon;
Spinning whose web of silken filaments,
Each, care-shelved, realized without alloy;
Days beatific—days exuding balm;
Quaffing, from hour to hour, whose nectared draughts;

Looting whose honey's store, each, toying, passed
In luxury.  Adverting, delegates,                           290
To object vital of our being convoked—
Warders of a protracted frontier-line,
We may, in course of the vicissitudes
Traced on past battle for the continent;
Whose echo still resounds, a waiting game
Have played ; shown vacillation—fickleness ;
Coquetted archly with the combatants.
Opposed we overtures for building forts,
As menaces to our ascendancy ;
So treating these, long frowned on compromise—
Deaf were to prayer alike of English and            301
Of French.  Evincing, p'r'aps, duplicity,
Our minds not always may, with guardedness,
Entry have barred for Jesuitic guile.
But now—since England sceptres Canada—
Should we our tribal countenance extend
To revolution, in collision we
Would come incessantly with border-tribes :
Delivered, then, our vote unanimous
To furnish fuel for that engine, which,              310
Over this western territory, would
Trample the sprite of shared authority.

    THAYENDANEGEA (*Spokesman for the Mohawks*).
Brothers of our robust alliance—you,

Connections valued from less blight-hung clime—
Reached is—try to conceal it as we may—
Tremendous crisis in our history :
Looms large athwart our pathway, sagamores,
Shape of the leering gnome of destiny !
If we may not elude, what effort should
We practise to retard, its chill embrace ?  320
Knot with the billet's mass incorporate,
Obstruct the Mohawks shall, with bribeless will,
Th' inserted wedge of smooth persuasion; while
Besetments parrying, with sense alert,
Of shrewd enticement, soft-keyed flattery,
With stores eked out from Circe's arsenal ;
Combat to latest gasp each agency,        [wrench :
Which from their customed moorings would them
Shall—watchmen at east door of the abode—
Scorn the coin minted to seduce their faith ;
Fling in the givers' teeth their subsidies.   330
For have there not repeatedly been flashed
Before us tokens of the fate we'll meet ;
Let but this set of throne-subverters, who
Law would uproot—tradition violate—
Such anarch clique attain predominance ?
Low conduct of the Dutch at Albany
(Some pillars of the new Republic) when—
Favoring the French—they strove to dispossess

Us of the fur-trade.   Promptly these the State   340
Its wholesome power put forth to circumvent.
With other things combined (extensive as
Uncheerful catalogue) to wake distrust;
Remembering, chiefs, that interregnum's stress,
To England; since her rule has ever been
Beneficent; because her liberal genius—
Her spirit tolerant—its seal impressed
On polity, which, through its processes,
Metes equity; I, their exponent, pledge,
Without reserve, my tribe's allegiance.   350

 Spokesman for the Cayugas.   Our lands imping-
  ing on the Senecas',
The grounds famed Sanguerachta doth accent
To mark their course, to us dictate
A like conclusion; his rehearsal clear—
Presentment as concise, as pertinent—
Action consentient from our tribe doth prompt.
Started in flight the arrow of my thought!

 Spokesman for the Onondagas.   From early
  dawn of the Confederacy,
To us, as keepers watchful—sedulous
Replenishers—of ancient Council-Fires,   360
The privilege of last-urged rhetoric
Belongs; not without zest we exercise
Right of propounding binding theories.

But since th' Oneidas—Tuscaroras (limbs
Of worth) have hither failed to congregate,
In force which might, with apt authority,
Permit them plainly to enunciate
Their tribes' positions, laid on us the need
At moment premature to intervene.
We're pleased at not being now constrained to state
Divergent doctrine ; make we common cause     371
With our associates. The strait demesnes
Of the Cayugas serving warningly
For western boundary ; their lake-starred home
Being eastern portal of the Senecas ;
With those safe claimants to hegemony,
The forceful Mohawks, at the farther east—
Oneidas, Tuscaroras, forming but
Illusive buffer—clearly we'd betray
Imperfect judgment, acting otherwise.     380
We can't omit this opportunity
To reason with those weak-kneed fellows—sprigs
Of the Oneidas, Tuscaroras ; would
Beg them a stiffer vein to cultivate :
Have them shake off their torpor, drowsiness ;
Be more than puppets—twitched automata ;
The urgency enforce—the seemliness—
Of coming forward speedily with help ;
On them the wisdom, duty inculcate

Of diligent contention in our cause. 390
'Ware all the lined palm of the recreants;
As idle make their craft, as when his gin
The fowler spreads within his victim's sight.
*[Exeunt omnes.*

SCENE 4.—PLACE: THAYENDANEGEA's *forest-camp near Unadilla.*

*Enter* THAYENDANEGEA *and* CANASTOTA.

THAYENDANEGEA. The forage-parties, Canastota,
I bade you raise to scour the pastures—have [which
You their report? You know our plight (is not
Our sum of tribulations openly
To *all* disclosed?) how as the piteous
Result of weary penning in the sour,
Infertile wilderness, whence we have late 400
Escaped, our patient warriors pinched are;
Enfeebled; famine-ground.

CANASTOTA. Their quest, I am
Apprised, has been rewarded by such haul
Of cattle as will tide us o'er the stress—
Amply relieve the hour's necessities.

*Enter a* Courier.

(*To Thay.*) Accept my salutations, powerful chief!
Despatched am I by General Herkimer—

He chairman chosen of the Committee
Of Safety for this hapless circuit.  His
Headquarters have been daily visited 410
By fluttered residents—weak settlers, whom
(All blindly guessing why 'tis introduced)
Your tribal strength dismays.  Him they implored,
With hurried breath, and mien aghast—their brains
A-reel, and nerves on rack ; with hueless cheeks
And quaking joints, to send a messenger
T'extract from you the reason of your braves'
Converging here in War's dyed panoply.
Names he in this (*handing a letter*) a certain rendez-
Where viands of discourse may be between     [vous;
You freely interchanged ; a suite of six, 421
At most, he with him brings ; that number he,
In fairness, thinks that yours should not exceed.

   THAY.  Do thou assure him I shall keep the tryst.
Convey from me atop of this demand
That those our fenceless brethren—Mohawks, who ;
When our more lusty scions last year faced
Toward Oswego, duressed were, in hopes
Of purchasing my inactivity,
Should be accorded prompt deliverance ; 430
Further, that Major Butler's family—
For him, at Albany, as sureties held—
Be free to join him at Niagara.

   [*Exit* COURIER, *and exeunt* THAY. *and* CAN. *severally.*

SCENE 5.—PLACE: *An open space near Unadilla—Encampment of* BRIGADIER-GENERAL HERKIMER.

TIME: *July 4th, 1777.*

GENERAL HERKIMER, COLONEL COX *and officers of the General's staff noticed in the foreground; an imposing force of militia found posted at a short distance from them.*

GEN. HERKIMER. Hail we this morn with rever-
The first inspiring anniversary     [ent acclaim,
Of beating out the precious lamina—
Fair scroll through which our sons repudiate
The helot-bondage of the Autocrat!
  COL. COX. All ranks shall quire the thankful
      chant. T' infuse
Into our breasts more fervid glow, 'tis told     440
That Gansevoort; when noised the rumor was
That he would be assailed from Canada;
Determining to be the earliest
To float the standard which the Congress had
Evolved—sore-driven for material—
Did Stanwix' frowning parapet adorn
With bunting, whose eccentric blend amazed:
Fashioned the emblem's parallels of stripes

Alternate of a soldier's cotton shirt,
And plump camp-woman's scarlet petticoat;   450
The clustered stars with deftness interweaved—
Their azure field from cloak of camelot.

 Gen. Herkimer.   Good troth, as admirable a dis-
Of spirited invention, as it seemed    [play
A burst of patriotic enterprise.   [sentiment—

 Col. Cox.   Defrayed the homage claimed from
I marvel Brant should show such backwardness,
In answering your rational request
For statement of the purport of his trip.

 Gen. H.   If I mistake not, the War-Captain comes.

(*Enter* Thayendanegea, *accompanied by* Captain
 William Johnson, Canastota, Bull, *and two
 other subordinate chiefs of the Mohawks.*)

Thayendanegea, sometime honored friend,  461
Well met!   Though we might you of tardiness
Accuse, the lapse from punctuality's
Condoned.

 Thayendanegea.   Inform me of the purpose, pray,
Of your inviting me thus loftily
To your encampment!

 Gen. Herkimer.    Just to do myself
The pleasure of renewing our disturbed
Acquaintance.

THAY.     Object highly plausible!
(*turning to the militia*)
This lowering array—have they, likewise,
In coming here, by kindred sentiments      470
Been actuated; all so amiably
Desirous the poor Indian to greet?
'Tis kind—extremely kind!
   GEN. HERKIMER.     But, seriously,
Good Brant, what benefit to you and yours
Hop'st to procure from their infatuate
Apparelling in Serfdom's livery—
Retention of the shackles it entails?
Are not you Tories playing all a losing game?
Inclined your anchors, are they not, to drag?
Find'st satisfaction—cheer—from your midnight
Surprise at Trenton (that aberrant form     481
Of Christmas box) wouldest for comfort, or
For solace to th' affair at Princeton turn—
That so ungracious New Year's after-clap?
   THAY.  On your own ground (for fender a cuirass
Of soldiery) 'tis laudable to twit!
Be not too sanguine of a prosperous
Conclusion to Rebellion's mad career.
Has its polluted stream so far pursued
A current equable?   Allowing that     490
In those incipient tussles German bands

Tasted misfortune; are they not by Howe's
Early successes easily outweighed ?
Solid the gains those arms retaliate.
Do not the legions of that General
With front invincible—cool doggedness—
From foothold in the Province still exclude
Your mainstay, Washington; from York's staunch
His so desponding, fagged battalions keep ?   [gates
Long Island—to which huddled rout lent I        500
My aidance; the White Plains—why these alone—
(Naught said of trend glimpsed though Burgoyne's
More than offset your meagre victories.   [advance)
On our side, also, of the sheet include
The vain diversion of Montgomery,
Against an unoffending Canada;
That courted failure—misthrown seed from which
*We* barned the sheaves; its author's fall—
Heroic all must grant—discomfiture,
Toilsome retreat of Arnold (soon submerged     510
The fame transcendent of the Kennebec)
Tail of the gaunt procession—apogee
Of the eclipse—recapture of Crown Point.

  Gen. H.   Interred those salient scraps of history—
Can you not, chieftain, otherwhere discern;
Are there not warnings chalked full legibly—
Staring Belshazzarean presages—

Of rapid downfall of your principles?
Attracted to our righteous flag have been
The backbone of the country—well-nigh all 520
Its sturdy yeomanry; rally around
Us, too, cream of the trading-populace.
Meanwhile, to strangle infant liberties,
Your King a pack of loutish Hessians,
Ignoble hirelings—without vestige they
Of nerving stake in the result—enlists.

   THAY. Fond viewer of the mote in brother's eye,
While lodged a beam in thine, that rusty piece
  Recoils. Misstep of your apostate sect
Such cant demolishes. For aliment 530
For the dwarf foundling, through sharp throes
    accouched,
Have not its nurses Prussia—Poland—milked?
Beholden are you not as almoner
To Lafayette; to whom, while helping him
To jam propitiatory, you've stretched the hand
Of unctuous fellowship; queer strap that binds
Louis-Seize gallants and *your* Demos crew.
A member, Herkimer, methinks, of a
Society of prideless pensioners
Comes feebly armed to read *that* homily— 540
Is scarcely qualified to lecture other folk
For errors such as you comment upon.

An antique proverb nicely fits the case :
People who live in tenements of glass
Could not be too unready to throw stones.
Travelling farther still afield—to lay
In rest polemic spears as yet unhurled—
Your courier presented my demands ?

 Gen. H.  So you remove your kin to nooks remote,
Compliance is conceded with that term.
With point that touches Butler's household, I 551
May, unassisted, not presume to deal.

 Thay.  Heap I on those first wants this supplement :
That our loved missionary, Stuart, who ;
Shunning its quicksand caves—cries out upon
The animosities—of politics,
Cessation know of treatment bowelless ;
Should respite have from rude espionage ;
Else option to migrate to Canada.

 Gen. H. He must attemper his enthusiasms ;
Refrain from intercession for the King : 561
Let him subscribe our articles, if he
Disbursings would of leniency acquire.

 Col. Cox (*to Gen. H.*).  Obliged are you not, General,
  to postpone
This sprightly duel ? Have you not engaged
Schuyler to meet to-day at Hartwick's Grant ?

Gen. H. (*to Thay.*). I am reminded, Brant, that other
Infringe upon our parley (we had looked     [calls
For your appearance here some days ago).
Would you object, then, to take up the thread    570
Of mutual converse, at identical
Hour on the morrow—at the self-same place?
   Thay. Howbeit, Herkimer, I can detect
No useful end that's served by lengthening
Our dialogue, I in th' arrangement broached
Am fain to acquiesce.
   Gen. H. (*offering his hand*). Part friends till then.
            [*Exeunt the hostile groups severally.*

SCENE 6.—Place: *Headquarters of* Gen.
   Herkimer—*the Commander's tent.*

*Enter* General Herkimer *and* Joseph Waggoner.

   Gen. Herkimer. I ask you, Waggoner, an
      enterprise
To shoulder which demands alertness; fund
Of circumspection; much cool-headedness.     579
   Joseph Waggoner. General, you may rely on me
Aught lying in weak man's capacity.     [to do
   Gen. H. Good henchman, there exists an absolute
Necessity to rid ourselves of Brant.

7

Could we the underpinning from beneath
The structure of the Indian compact sweep
(From first mad outbreak of the contest such
Thayandanegea has supplied) its fate
We might with fair approach to certainty
Predict.

    Jos. W. Should I in secret poniard him?
Charged such back-thrust with o'ermuch infamy! 590

    GEN. H. Tuggings of conscience must be disallowed.
Opinion of our Committee you know:
Resolved by them of vital consequence
To geld his energies by causing his arrest.
Why not apply the surer remedy?
Select with care, then, partners to assist
You in the deed's performance; have it come
To pass before the hour when we resume
Discussion: fitting means you must concoct.    599

    Jos W. Your mandate I'll fulfil; though—kept the
Salt of my manhood will be sacrificed.    [bond—

                  [*Exit* GEN. HERKIMER.
I dare not perpetrate this wickedness.
I'll find some way of sending word to Brant,
That he may have within convenient reach
Support such as would make it critical
In any wise to interfere with him.

                    [*Exit* JOSEPH WAGGONER.

SCENE 7.—Place: *The same as Scene 5.*

(*The several characters, with their attendants, discovered as before.*)

Thayendanegea. I've hither, Herkimer, returned
'Tis idle further to negotiate :   [to say
Honor—integrity—forbid that I
Should, in the slenderest particular,           610
Avoid the burden of the covenant
Which binds me to the British interest.
Sustained by living forces my regard ;
Twined with the fibres my ne'er bartered creed !
Schuyler too hastily consoled himself
With the belief that he had mesmerized
Our tribes, when were effusive belts exchanged
With them, two years ago, at Albany ;
Humored himself too far when he supposed
Their services—support—were vendible :       620
We with the English mean to sink or swim.
Our cantons feared not to stand out against
A State united ; shall we be deterred
From conflict, with such State cloven in two.
Unflinching may be your Bostonians ;
Yet shall King George completely humble them.

Col. Cox.  If such the chief's unalterable resolve,
Drowned, as result, I ween's our conference.
    Thay.  Ha! Colonel Cox plays us an interlude.
Are you not Klock, the trader's son-in-law ;    630
That juggling fleecer of our "planting-grounds"—
Splendid exemplar of maleficence :
A traffic founding upon human woes,
To doting braves dispenser liberal
Of the vile potion that inebriates ;
Those draughts pernicious which, unfailing, cloud—
Too oft dethrone—their reason ; which, with speed,
Annul their self-control ; which, presently,
Mad-slaying all the gentler, set ablaze
The baser, guiltier promptings, of their hearts ;    640
Through acts announced flagitious, bestial ;
The man transforming to insensate fiend ?
How flourishes the exile ?
    Col. Cox.           Should I here
Profess myself to be such relative,
What's that to you, accursèd Indian ;
Hankering for swill—lairing with feculence?

(THAYENDANEGEA *here gives vent to a whistle, which*
    *causes two or three hundred Indians to appear at*
    *the verge of the forest.*)

    Thay. (*to Gen. Herkimer*).  Rightly dost cower,
    reptile venomous !

Traitor detestable! not taunt alone,
With passion flung from yon low partisan
(Spite—ribaldry—I vow, which thy base heart 650
Approves) goad sharper than his insolence
Drave me to rouse those forest denizens.
The rather have I thus my might proclaimed;
Since thou, who call'st thyself a soldier; thou—
Pinnacled shepherd of the patriot flock
In these distracted borders—yestere'en
Didst stoop with hellish instinct to evolve
Dark plot to overpower—dispatch—me ere
Our ruptured palaver should be renewed.
Becomes thee well to wince—fall back abashed—
For had not one of those coarse myrmidons, 661
Whom thou hadst close-suborned to work thy will
(More tender than the chief conspirator)
Crept to me and divulged that black device
(Censure of his compeers how withering,
How stern, that decorous repentance breathed!)
Silenced, I trow, had been the tongue which now
Reviles thee.

 Gen. Herkimer. Disavow I cannot, chief,
Th' intention which provoked your outraged soul
To pour that lava-stream of contumely;
Aught urge that's like your heat to mollify. 670
My one plea for procedure, which you brand

As treachery, our party's exigence;
Belief that were the tribes abruptly torn
From your control; were they no longer bound
To the strained system of the Royalists,
By the tough girdle of your influence,
We might—if not for their secession look—
Persuade them to be neutrals in the strife.

   Thay. Most competent, i' faith, the casuist
Who his malfeasance *thus* would palliate!    680
When limberer code born of morality?
Though lawful fear of dimming your as yet
Unsmirched escutcheon as a child of Mars
Availed not to restrain from perfidy;
Spake not bright years of friendship—intercourse
Freely pursued, when almost joined our snug,
Our shaded farmsteads? Have those vintages
*All* scaped the wine-press? Herkimer, how should
Your bosom's ore endure the crucible?
Left vileness, guilt—left shame, impurity—    690
Light residue of flawless mineral!
Your bosom's growth what, after winnowing?
Binned rancor, hate—binned wrong, obliquity—
Spare quantity of clean, unrusted grain!

   Gen. H. Abuse—opprobrium—cannot recall
A dead transaction. But this prancing throng—

*(turning to the braves)*
Are they designed to serve as instruments
To point the blemish of the boomerang;
Which aimed has been awry—pitched clumsily—
By making me the victim of your ire?   700
 THAY. I tendered you that spectacle to show
I'm not a foeman to be trifled with;
Clearly to voice the truth that I possess
Resources that will justify my stay;
Should you compound not with us peaceably;
Should it not be accepted quietly,
*Compel* fulfilment of my mission here—
The victualling of my needy warriors.
But if so be withdrawal of my host
Disquiet should abate—expel alarm—   710
The note significant is uttered which
Will recommit them to their solitudes.

(THAYENDANEGEA *here sounds the signal of dispersal; to which his warriors yield instant obedience, by burying themselves, en masse, in the forest.*)

Coward! chew this for valedictory:
Their head you may somewhere, outside the range
Of your antipathies, confront again.
(*To Col. Cox.*) And as for thee, thou scurvy renegade,
In peace resume thy way—preserved to tell

Thy rosy children that the Indian,
Whom thou deridedst for his origin ;
*His* manners shutting out civility ;  720
Devoid *his* nature of right-mindedness ;
*His* morals drinking worst effluvia
(Let me not clip th' empoisoned diatribe)
*His* settled wont to torture and to flay ;
When thou wert placed within his savage clutch,
Returned thee to their arms unvexed—unharmed.
   [*Exeunt the hostile groups severally.*

END OF ACT III.

# ACT IV.

SCENE 1.—PLACE: *The Mohawk Valley — Forest near Oriskany.*

TIME: *August, 1777.*

*Enter* THAYENDANEGEA *and* MAJOR BUTLER.

   MAJOR BUTLER. Your military insight—fertile as
Sagacious proved—Thayendanegea, ought
To've led you, thoroughly to apprehend
The aim that underlay the policy
Of Germain; when he willed this arduous
Investment of Fort Stanwix. Following
His thrusting Arnold (with whose agileness,
Tenacity—whose martial fire—it tasked
Him to compete) from his vice-royalty;
Far-seeing Carleton, having by a show       10
Of masterly aggression—bright reward    [Point:
Of Valcour's bull-dog grapple—snatched Crown
As cheering first-fruits of Burgoyne's campaign,
By seizure of Ticonderoga capped—
Treat owed to the complaisance of St. Clair—
(The sundered continuity thereby

Restored was to the chain of gateways placed
Along the road to Canada) as much
Facilitating expeditions, 'twas
An article of equal moment held,           20
The series of passes to command
(Stanwix, of course, stout hinge upon the door
Of the great Carrying-Place) each loop control
Between Oswego and the Mohawk.  Chief,
For this St. Leger bowls his scorching sleet ;
For this his surly mastiffs fulminate.    [cied, would
   THAYENDANEGEA.  Such the reflections which, I fan-
Dictate—the move upon the Hudson (meant
New England to cut off from her supports)
The programme's corner-stone—our rulers' course.
Of motives which those rulers influenced,    31
In planning this ancillary attack,
Recounted *one* on which you laid much stress ;
As efficacy lending to conserve
Our country's prestige—longing to possess
Key of the noble Mohawk.  Butler, what
Huge sacrifices would we undergo
To save that beauteous inheritance
From fattening assets of the demagogues !
Sheet which—one's glance involving its whole track—
A grandeur scatters, sight-enravishing :      41
Banks wooded gloriously ; replaced, anon,

By scarpèd headlands—a surpassing, if
No plumb-line, masonry; Anthony's Nose,
Impressing by its knobbèd prominence,
With its saturnine profile—elegant
Pelisse of greenery; soft minister,
Which, now and then, with fructifying touch,
Cleaves opulent and quiet-nestling farms—
Refreshes (bland encroacher) scented mead;   50
Expanding here in reach pellucid—there
Wooing meek sprays of dipping foliage.
Those falls entrancing, riveting the view,
Near its debouchure; those in miniature—
Their basin tilèd with loose-tumbled rocks—
Which sparkle near my sometime home; its curves
Of outline exquisite; the princely train
Of purling tributaries which their lord
Attend.   Current that weds inconstancy;
Loitering in sullen depths; hurrying   60
In babbling shallows; calm—impetuous;
Discards a frolicsome abandon, but
To doze, peace-folded, in unfretting bed.

   Major B.   Most natural that keenness to uphold
Your title to such goodly legacy!

   Thay.   Discussing our immediate, pressing part
In pending ordeal—to here dismount
From Fancy's airy knolls—it looks as if

The hope which I expressed to Herkimer,
At Unadilla, that events some day 70
Might suffer me to bridge the chasmed space,
Destined to frown between our intercourse,
Would ear reach sooner than we then foresaw.
Turned the few leaves in volume of a month,
Since there transpired our so vivacious bout;
And now we're posted here, I learn, to balk
The plan he has in hand, with Tryon clowns,
To succor Gansevoort.
    MAJOR BUTLER. Guess not astray.
That dauntless, as industrious volunteer—
That wide-awake and capable vedette— 80
Your sister Molly, news of his approach,
In face of dangers formidable, vast,
With timeliness conveying to our camp,
St. Leger ordered Claus' Canadians—
The handful spared of Hanau riflemen—
My home-bred rangers, with your Indian
Auxiliaries, in haste to concentrate
At this advantaged spot to bar his way.
    THAY. Unfolded, truly, an exceptional
Locality to plant an ambuscade: 90
I have surveyed the ground; a deep ravine—
Its contour semicircular—from end
To end exhibiting a marshy bed;

Capacity sufficient to enclose
Manifold files, though they should choose to march
In broad formation; this tenèbrous gorge
(By causeway threaded of rough corduroy)
Invades his army's normal avenue
Of transit.   Overbrowing same, defined
Thick-garmented acclivities.   We could—          100
The progress of his troops impeded much
By dankness of the bog—a violent,
An irrecoverable blow inflict
Upon them from each curtained eminence.
Fair though seem the conditions so revealed;
While feasible to shut him in a trap;
Being far from satisfied the force told off
Is strong enough to cope with Herkimer,
I'll send a scouting-party to find out
His numbers and the form his column takes.          110
Defer we should, in any case—I would
Point out—th' intended harassment until
The rear-guard's head is entering the cleft—
The channel's blocked with sutlers' cumbrances.

   (*Sounds a whistle, and enter* CANASTOTA.) [mand;

   (*To Can.*)  Cull out a dozen braves from your com-
And pierce the thicket's tangle towards the east.
Get at, as nearly as you can, without
Betrayal of your hiding-place, the strength

And marching order of the enemy,
On learning this, with speed to us return.   120

> [*Exit* CANASTOTA, *and exeunt* THAYENDANEGEA *and* MAJOR BUTLER *at opposite sides of the stage.*

CANASTOTA *having completed his reconnaisance, and reported the relief-force as evidencing no marked disparity, as compared with their own, the detachment, in the position taken up, await the coming of the Provincials; upon whom, as soon as they arrive, a destructive assault is dealt by the combined media of musket and tomahawk.*

---

SCENE 2.—PLACE: *The Mohawk Valley — The British Encampment before Fort Stanwix.*

*Enter* THAYENDANEGEA *and* MAJOR BUTLER.

MAJOR BUTLER.  By virtue of our ready stratagem,
It, Brant, has certainly been given us
(To your wise handling of our dusk allies
Such fortunate result is mainly due)
The heedless enemy to decimate
Beyond our uttermost imaginings :
Five hundred men is their computed loss—
One-half of their militant following.

THAYENDANEGEA. Yet we have been no trivial
   sufferers.
Th' ensnarèd drove, after recovery           130
From the first wildering onslaught—source, moreo'er,
'Mong other ills, of hurt most desperate
To Major Watts (our sorest casualty)
Picked off a shoal of fighting Senecas;
Stroke which, I promise, will dissuade the rest
(Let Sanguerachta rate—coax smoothly—as
He may) from pressing forward to reduce
The fort. Counting, indeed, the booty grabbed
By Willett on his sally; equipage—
Sundry supplies—of Johnson's corps, I'd say    140
The honors were divided evenly.             [just

   MAJOR B. I fear the tidings, chieftain, we have
Received from friendly rangers of the wood
For *you* serves dish e'en less acceptable:
Word that your sister, wending towards her home—
But half-recruited from her onerous ride—
Was waylaid by Oneida turncoats; who
Her clothing stripped from her, her ornaments;
Then chased her to the Onondagas' bounds.

   THAY. When I'm no longer tied to service here,
But my own movements shall again direct,     151
That insult offered to Sir William's choice—
Atrocious slur upon his memory;

That cheapening of the family dignity—
The bravoes, trust me, Major, shall be made
To expiate by dole commensurate.

    MAJOR BUTLER. A prisoner taken near the action's
By Claus's men, reports that Herkimer     [close,
Exemplified true Spartan fortitude.
He, though he had been wounded cruelly     160
(His knee was shattered, and his charger slain,
At hottest season of the fusillade)
With saddle, at his wish, as staunchion leant
Against a tree; and smoking with *sangfroid*
His German pipe, direction of his troops
Declined to intermit.

    THAY.     His courage may, with full
Propriety, as sponge serve to efface
The purposed wrong I sorrowed to indict
Him for at fir-crowned Unadilla when
We met. Time, Butler, odd revenges brings;     170
My spleeny vilifier, Cox, was killed.

    MAJOR BUTLER. In his case, too, must ill-will be
    renounced.
                                                               [*Exeunt.*

SCENE 3.—Place: *Stillwater—near Saratoga.
Encampment of the Indians.*

A number of warriors are seen dragging violently, and
subjecting to general mal-treatment, Captain John
McKinstry, made prisoner by them as a result of
the engagement.

*Enter* Thayendanegea.

Thayendanegea (*addressing the captive*).
Dear friend, my soul is rent to find you here
Encompassed by so grievous danger; made
Torment's enlivening sport—selected as
The helpless butt for nauseous gibes; become
The shrinking victim of indignity.
   Capt. McKinstry. Your braves are unappeasably,
     I fear,
Enraged with me because my closed platoons—
When menaced by the riving tomahawk—     180
Discharged their fire so tellingly, that they
Dug cruel furrows in their rushing ranks.
   Thay. (*addressing the captors*).
Your prey, I charge you, warriors, to leave
Unharmed; you shall I amply compensate.
   *To* Capt. McKinstry.
Do not despair; you from the coils yet shall

8

I liberate which close entangle you.

*One of the captors.*
We itch to build the sacrificial pyre;
And though Thayendanegea loud entreat,
We shall no longer than first sunset wait        189
His locks to shear with our primed scalping-knives.
[*Exit* THAYENDANEGEA.

(*Left to themselves, the Indians, forming a ring about* McKINSTRY, *institute a death-dance; the harrowing effect of which for the prisoner is much enhanced by their indulgence in a succession of yells and gesticulations.*)

*Re-enter* THAYENDANEGEA.
Heed, warriors, my pleading utterance:
An ox which I and Ackland's officers
Have ta'en unusual trouble to provide,
Catching the glimmer of your camp-fires, treads
Securely tethered; savory barbecue
From its broiled flesh for you I prophesy.
Render to me your captive in exchange
Therefor; and on the hideless carcase glut
A less revolting, saner appetite.

*The warriors readily assent to the proposition; and the transfer takes place with mutual satisfaction.*
[*Exeunt omnes.*

SCENE 4.—PLACE: *The Mohawk Valley—Residence of Rudolph Shoemaker, a quondam King's Justice of the Peace, in the German Flats.*

A collection of Monarchists encircle LIEUTENANT WALTER BUTLER; who, at the moment, is making known, in animated tones, and with forcible gesture, the contents of an open letter (which he still holds in his hand) from three of the Royalists commanding before Fort Stanwix—SIR JOHN JOHNSON, COLONEL DANIEL CLAUS, and MAJOR JOHN BUTLER—to the inhabitants of the Valley at large. HON. YOST SCHUYLER is stationed near him, while two dozen or more soldiers—their arms laid aside—are lounging about the various corners of the apartment. The speaker has not finished his reading of the letter, when a detachment of the guard at Fort Dayton, under COLONEL WESTON, burst upon the company; and make prisoners of BUTLER and SCHUYLER. The rest of the party, including the contingent from Fort Stanwix, effect a disordered exodus from the room.

SCENE 5.—PLACE: *The Mohawk Valley—Headquarters of* MAJOR-GENERAL ARNOLD, *German Flats.*

Sittings of a Court-Martial composed of MAJOR-GENERAL ARNOLD, and three inferior officers of the Continental army.

*Enter from opposite sides* COLONEL MARINUS WILLETT (*Judge-Advocate*) *and* LIEUT. WALTER BUTLER *and* HON YOST SCHUYLER, *the two last-namd under escort as prisoners of war.*

COLONEL WILLETT (*addressing the Court*).
To face inquiry into—scourging know         200
For—their misdeed, I, seigniors, cite—impeach—
Before your worshipful tribunal two
Obnoxious King's-men ; the more dangerous
Being Walter Butler, he an officer
In "Butler's Rangers"—that feud-loving corps
Led by his famous father ; his ally
(Reported to have been the arch-knave's guide)
A certain Hon Yost Schuyler.  With a batch
Of graceless privies, they, the captured pair,
Communion held in secret at the house         210
Of Shoemaker ; who, scum unsavory,
Was early listed in His Majesty's
Commission of the Peace.  Of this advised,

Weston, swift-mustering quota of the guard,
Their séance did make bold to interrupt.
At moment of their advent, Butler stood,
Spicing with noisy speech a message, which
He brought, post-haste, from that triumvirate
Of Royalists before Fort Stanwix—his
(The prisoner's) father, Daniel Claus, Johnson    220
The baronet.  The screed they plundered.  It—
Vying with scorpion's virulence—adjured
The district to empower an embassage,
To be composed of individuals
Of note, to urge upon the garrison
The folly of resistance; stating fear
That—should they not assent—their Indians,
Exasperate—inflamed—by heavy loss
Encountered in that clash, when Greek met Greek
At red Oriskany, could by no tool    230
Of human handling—no persuasion—be
Withheld from venting their resentful wrath,
By dealing wholesale slaughter to the Vale.
Here 'tis—that masterpiece of devilry.

"Camp before Fort Stanwix,
"August 13, 1777.

" *To the inhabitants of Tryon County:*

"Notwithstanding the many and great injuries we have received in person and property at your hands; and, being at the head of victorious troops, we most ardently wish to have peace restored to this once happy country; to obtain which we are willing and desirous, upon a proper submission on your parts, to bury in oblivion all that is past; and hope that you are, or will be, convinced in the end that we were your friends and good advisers, and not such wicked, designing men as those who led you into error and almost total ruin. You have, no doubt, great reason to dread the resentment of the Indians, on account of the loss they sustained in the late action, and the mulish obstinacy of your troops in this garrison, who have no resources but in themselves; for which reasons the Indians declare that, if they do not surrender the garrison without further opposition, they will put every soul to death—not only the garrison, but the whole country, without any regard to age, sex, or friends—for which reason it is become your indispensable duty, as you must answer the consequences, to send a deputation of your principal people, to oblige them immediately to what, in a very little time, they must be forced—the surrender of the garrison; in which case we will engage, on the faith of Christians, to protect you from the violence of the Indians.

Surrounded as you are by victorious armies, one-half (if not the greater part) of the inhabitants friends to Government, without any resource, surely you cannot hesitate a moment to accept the terms proposed to you by friends and well-wishers to the country.

"JOHN JOHNSON,
"D. W. CLAUS, } *Superintendents.*"
"JOHN BUTLER,

COLONEL WILLETT *hands the communication to* ARNOLD; *who reads it aloud to the other members of the Court. Evidence being afterwards given, by those who assisted in securing the prisoners, to establish the Judge-Advocate's opening statement,* ARNOLD *addresses his colleagues.*

ARNOLD. Presentment hearing of the witnesses,
Observe you, colleagues, faintest scintilla
Of evidence, which could extenuate
This worm's depravity; mark anything
Which should the Court induce to moderate
Its punishment. (*The other members of the Court, having exchanged a few words with each other, now answer* ARNOLD.)
     In the award to him    240
Of recompense of death we all concur.

GENERAL ARNOLD (*addressing Butler*).
Night-faring trespasser upon our realm—
Dark emissary of the Brunswickites;
Moving within our lines, a suit to speed
That rules out the exemptions of a truce,
Have you, Lieutenant Butler, aught to urge
Against your sentence, in conformity
With military canons, as a spy?

LIEUT. BUTLER. I this submission with my
That I was busied with legitimate  [judges leave:
Problem of statecraft; acted simply as    251

The honest, if insistent, vehicle
For overtures to aid the Monarchy.

 Gen. Arnold. Plea less effective than ingenious.
This dread irruption of the savages;
Promised in case the so degrading cry
Of your superiors' manifesto should
Be not acceded to—should pass unheard;
Speaks through that baying of malevolence
The temper of the sober diplomat?   260
Reserved alone for soulless reprobate
Such frank brutality to champion.

 Lieut. B. 'Twas sought through the address to
For profit of the Valley's residents,  [intimate,
The feeling of the injured signers that,
In rightful notion of a crisis hard,
Yoked was their interest with their loyalty.

 Gen. Arnold. Your singular defence we do pro-
Untenable. Our judgment is that you [nounce
Have fully merited, and must endure   270
The extreme penalty.

 (*To the prisoner's escort*) The prisoner, guards,
Remove.           [worthiness

 (*To the Judge-Advocate*) Respecting the blame-
Of Schuyler need we to deliberate.

 (*At this point an urgent knocking is heard at the outer door; and an orderly is despatched to ascertain its cause. Returning, he makes this announcement to the Court.*)

ORDERLY. The mother of the prisoner Schuyler (waits
With her below his brother Nicholas)
Craves transient audience.

GEN. ARNOLD. Usher her up.

(ELIZABETH SCHUYLER, *being admitted to the room, casts herself, weeping, at* ARNOLD'S *feet.*)

ELIZ. SCHUYLER. Illustrious Arnold, giant of re-
Foremost proficient in the soldier's art— [source—
The urgings answer of a mother's plaint;
Convict not of unworth a mother's tears;     280
Anoint do thou with curing liniment
The aching sores—with pity's touch extract
The lance deep-bedded—in a mother's breast.
Badge-wearer, thou, of intrepidity!
Bends at your feet a grief-torn suppliant;
Pass not the fearsome edict—visit not
The crushing doom—upon my son, which doth
Involve the chiefer culprit.

GEN. ARNOLD. Dame, what ground
For clemency—right to the boon which you
In anguished accents, with dejectedness     290
Of soul—beseech, can you allege?

ELIZ. SCHUYLER.            The lad
(A mental weakling from his infancy)
Has not the wit—the fledged intelligence—
Thus to conspire to work you prejudice.

   COL. WILLETT.   I ask the Court t'indulge me if a
I interject.  This seeming simpleton         [word
Claims veneration from the redmen as
A seer—conceived's a person half-divine.
Could his imperious logic be applied
To plastic minds of Brant's fire-eating horde    300
Beleaguering Stanwix, by imparting some
Münchausen fable—rich-embroidered tale—
Of an o'erwhelming force which you conduct
Against their hive; used to successfully
Blind their perceptions, in some losing maze
Wove of misleading speech; as doth the sense
Of timorous gazelle the falcon cloud,
Ere it is stalked, we would, I warrant, make
Wise cession of the franchise of his life.

   GEN. ARNOLD (*addressing Hon Yost Schuyler*).
Schuyler, I'm told the aboriginal                310
Ascribes to you the wizard's prescience;
Endows you with his occult powers—his weird,
Unfleshly furniture.  Repair you, then,
With expedition to the British lines:
Instil into their swart irregulars,

By any form of conjuration, or
Of charmful spell which you can invocate—
(Whether you wave enchanter's wand, or should
Exert the necromancer's enginery,
We rate a thing of minor consequence)        320
The hardy fiction that I them pursue,
With wingèd phalanx, of resistless strength;
Pierce their credulity with any shaft
Stowed in your prophet's quiver. Dress this bait;
And we'll absolve your scandalous offence.

 Hon. Yost Schuyler. I do accept the terms;
  and shall put forth
My utmost efforts to attain the end
Desired.                                     [add

 Gen. Arnold. A shrewd Oneida will—a coat to
Of varnish to the frame—be sent with you.
We must, howe'er, exact security             330
That you the substance of the contract will
Perform.

 Mary S. A willing hostage for him, General,
Myself I tender.

 Gen. Arnold. Such arrangement we
Are indisposed to sanction; we require
One over whom our guards can exercise
A stricter oversight than we, without
Charge of oppression, could with you adopt.

Nich. S. Take me, I beg you, as her substitute.

Gen. Arnold. *That* stipulation's more agreeable.

Nich. S. (*to Arnold.*) Feeling convinced my brother
The ticklish business he here undertakes; [will fulfil
Till he—successful in the test—shall have          342
Achieved my ransom, and his credit saved,
Guard-room constraint shall lightly discompose—
Its gloom—its solitude—no whit appal.

Gen. Arnold. Detain him, guards, in grated cell
The outcome of his mission shall be learnt.    [until
                                              [*Exeunt omnes.*

---

SCENE 5.—Place: *Bivouac of the Six-Nations
before Fort Stanwix.*

A number of warriors are participating in a pow-wow.
  One of them, who has noticed Hon Yost Schuyler
  approaching, addresses him.

Indian Brave. Why hast our wigwams, Schuyler,
    sought—thou feat
Down-thrower of the future's barriers;
Intruder daring on her secrecy?                    350

Hon Yost Schuyler. Hearken, dull votaries of
Power unresponsive, puny arbiter;        [Manitou—
Peoplers of Fetishism's swales unsunned,
Can naught pierce your obtuseness—lift the film?
Leaning upon impotent Deities,

In vain you hunger for *their* avatar:
Confiders in a disciplineless Chance;
Deign ye to reckon with realities.
In number as the pebbles strewn upon
Oneida's shingly beach, or as th' uncombed,       360
Dun-crested giants of these hoary woods,
The hosts of Arnold dog you.   Maybe, you
Would still insist on testimony, which
Should eye-arresting be, and palpable?
Is't not supplied?   Examine well my coat—
Gnawed as it is by shot; frank souvenirs
Which emanate from vaward skirmishers;
Escape unmaimed from whose so searching hail
Would nothing short seem of miraculous.
*His* flaming sword advanced; if, murmurers, you
(Depressed as is your passions' mercury,       371
To notch more low must slide the register)
Would your undoing by due forethought stave—
If you would ruin irretrievable
Avoid—no loophole's visible, except
To Geneseo a confused stampede.
               [*Exit* Hon Yost Schuyler.

*The Indians, upon this announcement being made, break up their conference; and, dispersing in different directions, circulate the disastrous news throughout the camp.*

SCENE 6.—Place: *Cherry Valley—Residence of Robert Wells; Headquarters of* Colonel Alden.

Time: *November, 1778.*

*Enter* Col. Alden *and* Susan Campbell.

Susan Campbell. The women, Colonel, of our
    district have
Robed me with credence of a delegate,
To drill into your sceptic intellect
What seems to them most bodeful prospect—this,
That Walter Butler, chafing under sting       381
Of his imprisonment at Albany
(Just pain to which he was remitted, as
Commuted sentence knelled by Arnold, which
His life pronouncèd forfeit as a spy;
And all too soon abridged by his escape)
With host descends of blood-crazed savages
Upon our homesteads. Wherefore, they request—
Beseech—you to afford them liberty
To store the costlier of their portable       390
Household effects within the walls secure—
The strengthful hedge behind of palisades—
Which screen our guardians. I, furthermore,
Disburden wish that you will not forbid
Their resting in that haven over-night.

Col. Alden.  I hold the danger quite chimerical.
It cannot be that parties so remote
As Stanwix ('twas from there the ruffling news
Has come) should be possessed of definite
Idea of the purpose of his move.             400
The situation certainly does not
Necessitate the transfer of your goods;
Nor yet the sheltering lodgment which you ask.
The fort, besides, could not accommodate
All comers; and, in such a matter, I
Would have to banish partiality.
Content you: I have set a careful watch;
Cordoned the neighborhood with lynx-eyed scouts.
This should suffice to dissipate alarm.       409
    Susan Campbell.  Grant that a false security do
Yourself and others in th' abysm hurl!        [not
              [*Exit* Susan Campbell.

    Col. Alden.  Have I been hasty in discrediting
These glum reports? Yet why should Butler pick
Upon *our* settlement to eke his spite?
Nevertheless, he might so act because
We are the thickest-peopled, most exposed—
The fairest—hamlet by Otsego's strand.
     (*Notices a horse and rider approaching.*)
Why spurs this horseman hither in such haste?
A look it has of evil augury.                 419

(*Enter* DAVID HAMBLE, *a countryman.*)

DAVID HAMBLE. Fly, Colonel, and acquaint the
Batter the redskins at your very gates.   [garrison!
Though not before receiving wound acute,
I slipped the demons scarce two miles from hence;
The sweat diffused about my horse's flanks—
His heaving chest, and wide-distended eye—
Are witnesses of the rapidity
With which th' unwelcome tidings have been borne.
'Tis hinted that the sentinels, assigned
The region whence the rout emerged to scan—
Lax estimate forming of their employ—      430
Were captured by them, sleeping at their post.
                              [*Exit* HAMBLE.

COL. ALDEN, *on receiving this intelligence, starts at once for the fort; but, being overtaken by the advance guard of the Indians, is ruthlessly scalped.*

SCENE 7.—PLACE: *The same—Apartment in a farm-house.*

The matron of the house, ALICE LINDESAY, is found employed in domestic work; a couple of children observed playing about her.

*Enter* THAYENDANEGEA.

THAYENDANEGEA.   Unrecking, senseless woman,
   stopp'st within

This flimsy sanctuary, calm, unawed;
In doom-vowed dwelling, unprotected, dost
Concern thyself with stale domestic cares,
While friends—relations—are being massacred?

    ALICE LINDESAY. Stands one in jeopardy that
        owns the King?

    THAY. That plea I fear 's of small avail to-day—
Prefers but fragile reed on which to lean.
I tried to warn—so save from butchery—      440
The Wellses; love-knit, blameless circle theirs,
To buy whose safety I'd have forfeited
My life. Inimical, alas, the fates!
Aiming the spoilers to anticipate,
I chose a nearer path; (tale pitiful!)
The ropy mire oppressing the nude fields—
'Gainst passage steely bent on laying an
Embargo—clasped my plunging limbs, with grip
Of ooze-fouled tentacles. This so prolonged
My journey as to make it vain; else had      450
I carried been upon electric wing,
To obviate their thrilling agonies;
Deliver saints from grisly martyrdom.
Slain, too, the helpmeet of your minister;
And all the number of poor Mitchell's brood.

    ALICE LINDESAY. Doth Joseph Brant not lead the
Where issue casts from dies of adamant,    [Indians;

Apostle, he, of gracious clemency;
Foe chivalrous, who—albe sorely clogged,
In brave endeavors to be merciful, 460
By bristling stubble dark propensities
Of underlings protrude upon his path—
Oft lifting arm humane, the murderous blow
Deflects ? Have you not heard how he did thrice,
With grand outgoing of benignity,
In awninged wilds keep watch o'er woe-racked knots
Of women refugees, to hinder blasts
Of harm ? Were he but here, I might dismiss
All fear.

 THAY. 'Tis Joseph Brant who speaks. 470

 ALICE LINDESAY.      The Heavens
Be praised!

 THAY.  I would not damp your hopes; but I
Enjoy, pressed hare, subordinate command—
Joining with Captain Butler in his raid
Reluctantly; consented only, when,
By reasoning gainsayless, I grew convinced
That my mere presence 'mong my followers
Would tend to keep them from uncurbed excess.
While conscious of wide limit to my power;
Of movements handicapped—of impulses 480
Repressed—do will I, sister, all I can
To spare you outrage; injury avert
From lambs about you tender, delicate.

Nor is there time to lose; for I descry
A file hard by of tigerish Senecas,
Eager to try the temper of their claws.

(THAYENDANEGEA *here sounds a keen whistle, which
is responded to by a number of Mohawks.*)

(*To one of the braves.*)
Here, paint at once, in clear-drawn characters,
My totem's sign upon these innocents.

(*The warrior, as commanded, traces, one after another,
a rough representation of a wolf on the fore-
heads of the woman and her children.*)

(*To* ALICE LINDESAY.)
Arrange yourself, without delay, in bed;
And when the vultures shall invade the room,   490
Symptoms of illness aptly simulate.
Perceiving this; together with my mark—
Interpreting its import, as of yore
Was done with smear upon the lintel—they
Will leave, I know, without molesting you.

[*Exit* THAYENDANEGEA.

*The Senecas here break into the chamber, with every
manifestation of hatred and fury; but, noticing the
apparently suffering woman, and their War-captain's
device imprinted upon her and the children, refrain
from offering them violence, and leave the house.*

END OF ACT IV.

# ACT V.

SCENE 1.—PLACE: *Battle-field of the Minisink.*

TIME: *July, 1779.*

Into the presence of THAYENDANEGEA is roughly haled, by half a dozen warriors, MAJOR WOOD, freshly captured by them in the fight.

MAJOR WOOD (*addressing Thayendanegea*).
Illustrious and puissant chieftain, thou,
Who striven hast to minish—aim'st to check—
Th' ensanguined flood, which scarce doth intermit
To drench and stain the bosom of this once
Bright-featured, smiling, fruitful; but now soiled,
Deflowered—now scourged and lacerated land;
Zealous hast wrought, through exercise of arts
Of dexterous and winning suasion, or
By force of just, yet temperate, reproof,
To free the frozen rills which manacle—confine— 10
Each wholesome and each righteous impulse; pierce
The sealèd pores that exit long have blocked
For every charitable feeling, of men's hearts; [kindly
(Grace-founts dried up—good dictates gagged—

Sensation indurated and benumbed)
The savor of whose broad humanity
Helps cleanse the murk—from horror absolute
Redeems th' outrageous frenzy of the times;
The chronicle of whose so ruthful deeds,
Throwing bright beam the stage across of War's   20
Remorseless havoc—o'er the lurid track
Of Ruin's scathing tempest—softens, dulls
The blenching vision ever being preferred—
Painting for us in horrid surfeit limned—
The writhing heap which sinks beneath the heel
Of deathful carnage—those disfigured forms,
Which daily, hourly, fill the needy maw
Of that foul gourmand—raise, benignant foe,
Thy saving arm, and snatch me from these ghouls!

    Thay. System I might be willing to adopt,   30
Which interfere should with my warriors'
Control of prizes gained by them in war
(Thought of as their distinctive perquisite)
Would breach their spirit of obedience;
Favor the sapping the authority
Essential found to their efficiency:
Breeding in them a fractious sullenness,
Purvey apt tinder for a mutiny.         [ment—

    Major Wood. Chief, mightier, more moving argu-
Should trite entreaty serve not to awake   40

Compassion—higher, holier appeal
Lags in reserve. Behold the token's passed ;

*(Frames the Master-Mason's grand hailing-signal of
   distress)*

That excerpt from a magic alphabet ;
Which, wheresoever radiates the strength
Of our august, protecting brotherhood ;
Extends the virtue of the talisman—
The blessing travels of the cordial ;
When flashed it is by suitor—one forlorn,
Necessitous ; anchored its spreading pale
Within, plenteous indulgence, comfort—grace—  50
For him assures ; succor, relief, if begged,
Procures, instant—unquestioning—from his
More prosperous fellow.

 Thay.     Open not to me
*That* potent prayer to brush aside ; your true-
Aimed shot brings down the hunted game ; attests
That chance-loosed barb an errless archery.

 (*To the captors.*) Braves, 'tis my will your captive
  be released !

          [*Exeunt omnes.*

SCENE 2.—PLACE: *Near Harpersfield, on the east branch of the Susquehanna.*

TIME: *April, 1780.*

A Provincial scouting-party of fourteen persons, under the leadership of LIEUTENANT ALEXANDER HARPER, found established in the woods, occupied with sugar-making.

LIEUT. HARPER (*to the rank and file of the party*).
Men, our commission may be brief rehearsed:
The commandant of the Schoharie Forts—
Bluff Colonel Vrooman—has our squad detailed,  60
T' ascend to sources of the Delaware;
With bold intent to learn the projects—watch
The panther movements—of the savages.
While this prime object of our errand, we
Have been enjoined, by way of incident,
(So winning prized addition to his stores)
To lose no fitting opportunity
The maple's toothsome produce to extort:
With weather of such quality as tends
To crown with profit our experiments—  70
The genial sun a forcing-pump by day,
A kind usurper's reign the night's crisp frosts—
Pursuit we prosecute with heartiness.

Still would I safer feel, if certified
(In days of soon-dispelled serenity,
We, sturdy woodsmen, sportive school-mates were)
Of the unloved marauder's whereabouts.
The man would seem to be ubiquitous;
In his sporadic visitations, will
Smite Middleburgh—pounce on the "Butternuts;"
Burst out at Springfield—startle Cobuskill.     81
Recurs a spicy legend of these parts,
Which him identifies with lively play
Upon his name.   Captain McKean—his friend
Before the troubles—summoned to repel
A foray; finding that the chief had just
Removed from quarter, where he had designed
To test his mettle, to a point not far
Away; but that he purposed to return
At night, prepared a high-flown challenge; which
He straight exposed upon an Indian trail;     91
Scrawling thereon—to rub his foeman up—
That he had "oft proclaimed himself a *man;*
But if he'd deign the tree-pinned gage t' accept,
To level would he of a *Brant-goose* sink."
Mention of Colonel Vrooman brings to mind,
Brant's treatment of a namesake; which bears out
The judgment bruited of his lenity;
While with the other showing ludicrous

Compliance with behest (expedient hatched 100
To yield him freedom) which, 'twas hoped,
He—suiting to his need—would contravene.
He had been captured by the sachem's braves;
And—motioned to a patch of woodland, at
Short distance from their wigwams, to collect
Some bark—the dullard, gibbeting his chance,
Raced back with the superfluous article.

(*At this point,* THAYENDANEGEA, *at the head of forty Indians and ten whites, dashes into the centre of the group; two of whom the band despatch before the chief can interfere.* THAYENDANEGEA *himself, feigning intense ferocity, rushes upon* HARPER, *with uplifted tomahawk.*)

THAY. Harper, while filled with genuine regret
At our rencounter; my poised axe must cleave
Your skull—rip ope your flesh—unless you shall
Divulge the number of the soldiery 111
(If so be any regulars contain)
At present manning the Schoharie Forts.
I caution you 'gainst practising deceit;
For whatsoever estimate you may
Conclude to give, I can depute a scout
Its truth to verify. Leisure you will
Enjoy, in such event, to speculate

Upon the doom you will incur, should yours
Agree not closely with my messenger's;  120
Should wear the stencil-print of falsity.

   LIEUT. HARPER.  Chief, fearing that you might be
About our skirts; impatient to expend    [hovering
Your desolating vigor on our hearths—
Re-light your charring furnace on our plains—
We were allowed three hundred men, with which
T' effectually frustrate your pillagings.

   THAY.  In dealing with my operations, you
No overplus betray of modesty;
However, I suppose I must accept  130
That plain averment : still, it may not glad
Your ears to learn that, since my enterprise
Abortive proves, our slackened steps diverge
Toward the west —their goal Niagara :
A tramp at no time fraught with blissfulness;
Intolerable for hampered prisoners.

*The prisoners now (with the exception of Harper) whose rank exempts him from the humiliation—with heavy packs strapped upon their backs—commence their dolorous and weary trudge to Fort Niagara.*

SCENE 3.—Place: *The vicinity of Tioga Point— near the confluence of the Susquehanna and the Chemung.*

A company of ten savages—a portion of Thayendanegea's predatory band—having in custody five white prisoners, three men and two children—collected around their camp-fire in the woods. Two forked stakes are seen secured in the earth, one on each side of the fire; and placed between them (resting on the forks) two poles, against which the warriors' rifles are leaning. These are occupied in roasting the flesh for their evening meal; when one of them—the operation completed—lays his knife upon the ground, near the feet of Van Campen, one of the prisoners (the arms of all of whom had been firmly pinioned) who, observing the act, covers it at once with his foot, without the movement being detected by any of the Indians. A short time only elapses before the Indians address themselves to sleep; five of them disposed on either side of the fire—their heads under the poles, and the rifle of each in position to be grasped upon the instant. Van Campen now sits up; and, peering out, endeavors to ascertain if all are asleep; a truth of which he becomes assured by the snoring of the savages. Having with his foot drawn the knife within reach of his shackled hand; he — rising cautiously —rouses his companions, Pence and Pike. Pence promptly cuts the bands girding Van Campen; who, in turn, sunders those of his comrades. They then remove all the rifles to a tree, at a short distance from the fire, (depriving their captors, at the same time, of their tomahawks) both acts being performed without awaking any of them. VAN CAMPEN, with a tomahawk, quickly dashes out the brains of one of the Indians on the right side of the fire; but PIKE, who had been expected to accomplish the destruction of another in the line, draws back on his intended victim's venting an alarming "ugh;" and extending his arm, as though to seize his rifle. VAN CAMPEN, however, seeing him stir, with lightning rapidity drives his tomahawk through the Indian's head; a performance he repeats with the remaining savages on his side of the fire. PENCE, at this juncture, fires the second of the three rifles of which he had possessed himself (the first essay had resulted in a flash of the pan) the charge passing through the heads of four of the Indians arranged on PENCE's side of the fire. The fifth, CANASTOTA, aroused by the ring of the rifle, bounds to his feet, and rushes towards the spot where the fire-arms had been stacked over-night. VAN CAMPEN darts between him and the tree; and CANASTOTA turns in flight. VAN CAMPEN, pursuing him, splits his shoulder with his tomahawk; CANASTOTA, here grasping his adversary, they both fall to the ground, VAN CAMPEN underneath. They strain together with unrelaxed nerve, each writhing to break free. VAN CAMPEN, lying under CANASTOTA's maimed shoulder, is almost suffocated by the blood which streams from the latter's wound. The tomahawk at this point dropping from him, he stretches his hand around CANASTOTA'S body to reach his knife; but the Indian's belt having become twisted round his waist when they first fell, he finds it to be beyond his grasp. At length, springing to their feet, they wrench themselves apart. VAN CAMPEN seizes the tomahawk; but CANASTOTA, taking to flight, passes beyond range.

---

SCENE 4.—PLACE: *Tioga Point.*

THAYENDANEGEA *and his detachment in camp.*

*Enter* CANASTOTA.

THAYENDANEGEA.  Com'st, Canastota, to the
Untended by a single warrior?  [rendezvous,
  CANASTOTA.  All, save myself, redoubted chief,
By you sent forth to rake for spoil, became  [of those,
The victims of a sickening tragedy.
Beyond the waters of the Delaware—
In breeze-swept highlands of the Minisink—
We took five prisoners—convoy numbering
Three men, two children.  At the outset, we
Were careful to abstract such articles
From them as might be used to our despite;
Or, peradventure, simplify escape:
Nor did neglect to fetter them at night,

One of our party must, unthinkingly, 150
Have dropped his knife, when roasted was his meat;
Forgetting stupidly to repossess
Himself of it thereafter: some alert
Intelligence among the captives, then—
Watching its chance—the weapon, probably,
Secured, when we our frames surrenderèd
(The forest-floor for snow-hemmed palliasse)
Leased was our consciousness—to earned repose:
With it effecting severance of our bonds.
For I was shook from slumber's vise-like hold 160
By piercing crack of rifle (they had reft
Us of our lethal wares) whose deft discharge—
Their figures in alignment luckless ranged—
Four warriors sped; gashes from tomahawk
Successively five others' pulses stilled;
Leaving these thews alone to withstand Death;
Leaving these veins alone by him unchilled:
From whose all-mangling talons I myself,
After a surging conflict, disengaged.

(*Showing them nine pairs of moccasins.*)
Gaze, clansmen, on these moccasins—full eloquent
Mementos of companions you have lost! 171

   *Warriors in concert.* The pale-face captives tor-
      ture—mutilate! [tune—
CAN. You, fellow-braves, with warmth I impor-

With earnestness; relinquish your resolve.
Be more fair-minded; show yourselves to be
Dispassionate; in this untoward affair
Act ye more noble—honorable—part.
Comrades! unskeined my doleful narrative,
But to explain why you in me behold
Pathetic remnant of our stalwart band;   180
Not to excite your feelings—bellows plied
Not to inflame to murder.  Chargeable
In no way upon *these* that holocaust;
No baneful privity of will was theirs
In its iniquity: their hands in your—
In my—kinspeople's blood was not imbrued.

THAY.  Deny not, warriors, his fair desert
To Mercy's advocate; those lessoning lips
Judicious lore distil; with Justice is
Their sentence consonant.  Train they upon   190
Us Reason's batteries.  The tapping guest
Admit.  Dip, braves, in Pity's flowing well:
Stable Revenge.  Let the thaw liquefy
The icicle; do not, I you implore,
With wanton crime your consciences o'erload.

*As a result of these appeals, the warriors renounce their intention of avenging their comrades' deaths upon the prisoners; and both prisoners and captors resume their march.*

SCENE 5.—*Geneseo.*

*Enter* THAYENDANEGEA.

THAY. Twice have the captives been from slaughter
Once (hard upon their taking) when I found [spared:
It such an uphill task to overrule
My warriors' protest that the maintenance
Of such a troop, with our reduced supply     200
Of food, would be unfairly onerous;
Next, when extinction lit (in purlieus that
Where feasts the eye on Susquehanna's plumed
Sublimity) on Mohawk's hapless nine.
Were they preserved from peril so immense;
Rescued with pain from pass so terrible:
Have they been helped, at hazard, twice to burst
Fate's circling trammels—dodge the shadowing,
Stern Nemesis, which sought—lewd cormorant—
In guiltless tissues to infix her beak;     210
Have they outlived that crowning misery—
Compulsion laid upon them to subsist
For haggard days on putrid horse-flesh (dread
Privation we, too, shared) but to succumb
To spiteful buffets from the gauntlet-files,
Still to be met, expectantly arrayed,
Between this station and Niagara?

I have not judged it proper to confide
To Harper sequel of his niece—Jane Moore's—
Abduction from her Cherry Valley nest          220
(Rifling without my knowledge, privity)
How Captain Powell, vested with command
At Fort Niagara; when she had been
Entrusted to the warden's custody,
After an ardent courtship, married her.
I'll send a runner forward to suggest
To Powell to arrange festivities
(Naming the Nine-Mile Landing on the Lake)
For both encampments of the Senecas,
Established in the Fort's vicinity.            230
The braves decoyed—the prisoners should the test,
Dealt by the feebler Amazons, surmount.

*(Sounds a signal, in answer to which a Mohawk
brave appears.)*

With this (*handing him paper*) apace make for
To Captain Powell's self deliver it.           [Niagara;

SCENE 6.—PLACE: *Cleared ground adjoining Fort Niagara.*

A number of Indian women and boys found marshalled in column, *vis-a-vis*, armed with various kinds of offensive weapons. THAYENDANEGEA'S captives, at the highest speed of which they are capable, dart through the gap, so formed; all, with the exception of one, who is struck down by an unusually muscular blow from one of the termagants, but recovers himself, and resumes his flight, gaining the farther outlet of the defile in safety.

---

SCENE 7.—PLACE: *British America*—THAYENDA-NEGEA'S *home, at New Oswego, on the Grand River.*

TIME: *1788.*

*Enter* THAYENDANEGEA *and* COLONEL JOHN BUTLER.

THAYENDANEGEA.   The clamor, Colonel, that the Miamis,
The Wyandots—and tribes with them affined—
Have vented steadily, persistently;
Since the conclusion of the treaty which
Acknowledged th' independence of the States;
Caused by intrusion of the frontiersmen             240
On lands they cling to—lands they represent
As being secured to them by guarantee—
Grows every day more loud, more blustering;

Th' alarum, deafening in its resonance,
Salutes the Commonweal defiantly.           [domain,
   Col. Butler.  As feature which delimits their
They claim, with iterance, Ohio's stream;
Beyond that waterway the truculent
Backwoodsman drives them unrelentingly.
   Thay.  Before dissension reached its present height,
The Senecas' magnetic orator—                           251
Red Jacket—had inflamed them mightily.
*He* would revive the dream of Pontiac;
Through a cementing of those looser tribes
By arms to subjugate the continent.
Th' upheaval, Butler, has significance
For the Six-Nations; since the sovereigns
Of those far kingdoms—reckoned such with pride
Their ancient patrimony; the aroused,
Sore-agitated subjects of these wrongs                  260
Angle for the support of our depressed—
Our almost water-logged—confederacy;
Want me as intermediary to draw
My faint, afflicted countrymen—as well
As those their offshoots by St. Lawrence found—
Into the maelstrom of their enmities.      [Should I
   Col. B.  How construed, chieftain, your remarks?
Conclude from them that you these plaining tribes'
Advances are averse to entertain?

You have not always blamed their policy;  270
Nor with repugnance its maturing marked.
  THAY.  Colonel, I candidly confess that I
At one time countenanced aggressive steps;
But while (as ever) zealous to denounce
The malice fostered—the injustice done—
Procrustes' *alter ego*, Circumstance;
Prostrate upon whose couch—Man's Life—have all
To its manipulation to submit,
Did more pacific feeling generate.
What could we gain through the entanglement?
How would our aid, our service be recouped?  281
Vested in us by parchment, under seal
Of Haldimand, the tenure of demesnes
Of large extent—potential opulence.
Why should we recklessly endanger their
Possession, by our entry meddlesome
On quarrel which the King; although he still
Retains in pawn th' outlying fortresses—
Largely because it serves as stimulant
To the secessionists to ratify  290
Their pledges to these Indians—disapproves?
Better the ferment to accommodate.
Our worldly stock, once carried to the pound,
Could we, with hope, for its redemption look?
The concept with imprudence is replete;

Their project's leaky ship, if it leave port,
Will take big cargo of foolhardiness.

   Col. Butler.  I think with you it could not but
A scaling of the topmost altitude     [denote
Of folly to oppose their feebleness—     300
Their noted dearth of war-material—
To our proud neighbor's wealth; match these against
His ingenuity, cohesive strength—
Girt this with buckler in the confidence
Accruing in Experience's school.
Should, then, a rising haplessly ensue,
Insure it must its own futility.

   Thay.  Before the close of navigation, I—
Redeeming written promise that I gave—
Sail for Detroit; there striving in debate     310
With speakers chosen by the Miamis
(They, with the Shawanese and Kickapoos,
Are hot for war, whereas the Delawares,
The Pottawatomies and Chippewas,
The Ottawas seem predisposed to peace)
When I shall not alone decline to lend
My people's sinews to enlarge the rift;
But urge my froward fellows to discard
An attitude, which surely must for them     319
The march accelerate of destiny.     [address—

   Col. B.  With your self-balance—consummate

You must with them yourself ingratiate.
Whilst I would be—to strand unwind from yarn
Of prophecy—prone, chieftain, to affirm,
That were it not your cue to reconcile,
But rather to engage in the affray,
Your operations could not but enhance—
Root durably—your enviable repute
As one deep-learned in warfare's subtleties;
Much gratified am I to know that you,                330
During your sojourn in the mother-land,
Developed less hard-metalled aptitudes;
While there, the sugared cates of Fame partook—
None of the adulation missed—which form
The gilt oblation of Society.
Will you—as light refection for the brain—
A pasty knead of those frivolities?            [hand—
    THAY. First, then—desired to kiss King George's
I was excused from the performance, when,
(Rail at me for a cheerful egotist)                340
I did, assuming air of stateliness,
Give out that I a reverenced sovereign was
In my own realm; presumption packed in which
Tall flourish I essayed to mitigate,
By an ingenuous offer to enact
Like graceful tableau with the Queen Charlotte.
Succeeded hap tinged with some gravity;

When masque I graced in toggery of Mars.
The Sultan's maladroit ambassador,
Affecting to be highly sceptical                350
Of my face-pigment's being a true vermeil;
No sanction pleaded from Byzantium,
T' explore my nose made gesture tentative.
I straight restored him to demeanor staid;
Upset the fair sex' equanimity,
By vicious swinging of my tomahawk.
I chummed with Boswell; joked with Fox;
Grew intimate with sparkling Sheridan;
The friendship gained of philippizing Burke:
Challenged the public gaze, in general.          360
                              [*Exeunt.*

---

SCENE 8.—PLACE: *Indian Agency at Detroit—an assembly of North-Western Indians in convention.*

TIME: 1788.

*Enter* THAYENDANEGEA *and a chief of the Miamis.*

MIAMI CHIEF. We one recourse, Thayendanegea,
With our petition to you to extend       [have,
Our hard-pressed league your tried adherents' help
In their adversity (through our complaint
Is voiced the Chippewas', the Delawares',
The Ottawas', Shawanese', Kickapoos',
The Pottawatomies) *this* to address

Your sense of racial pride and dignity;
The heart-strings finger of the patriot.
With obligations twisted; treaties cracked—
The tonsure practised on their sanctity;  371
With faith proscribed—of right oblivious—
Scoffed at, rode over rough-shod are our claims:
Their honor flown—seared their humanity—
Our welfare's blasted, marred our happiness;
Cheated are we of comfort, as bereft
Of ease; subsistence—*life* is jeopardized,  [cupidity.
Through "Long Knives'" hate, "Long Knives'"
They covet everything which we can boast;
Estates—the stinted substance—we enjoy.  380
The lands that hug Ohio's western rim,
'Tis urged, forsooth, are much too valuable—
The rolling pastures by its affluents,
The Wabash, the Scioto, fertilized—
Too broad, accessible, for us to hold:
Hie, therefore, to the western wilderness
We must to seek a ruder, meaner home!
Hunted—are we to passively submit?
Plundered, despoiled, shall we remain content?
With folded arms look on, and see  390
Our treasured properties—our goods—absorbed?
Lie by, with torpid unconcern, to find
Swallowed the vails of faithful husbandry;

The hardships felt—the travail borne—by us
As pioneers disclaimed? Poltroons, shall we
Permit the sweetened ties, which birth upon
The soil begets—the fire-side consecrates—
To go unpriced, unweighed: attachments—hopes—
Make no attempt to rescue these from blight?    399

 Thay.   Courageous champion of an honored line!
Whilst I commiserate your cheerless lot;
Indignantly revolve those grievances,
Which you delineate so touchingly;
Jealous trustee of others' interests,
Less amply dowered with judgment—less
Securely cased in wisdom's armoury—
I scarce could be expected to embark
On venture, that would fatefully commit
My not unworried fold to course, which wombs
A stake momentous, without its assay    410
By Reason's probe; without dependence placed
On her informing plummet's cast.   I, chief—
So sifted; from its bran of fatuousness,
Bolting the niggard flour of sanity,
Impugn (I knew beforehand that you aimed
At war) your remedy; frankly pronouncing it
As ill-judged, as it is unpromising.
Can you, with your sparse numbers—weak resource—
Hope to prevail against the thirteen States,

Their armies trained—their deadly implements?
Be not deluded into fancying 421
The King doth conjoint action meditate.
With promptness, friend, quit *that* Fool's Paradise!
Indifferent, nor callous would I seem—
Yet th' armed assistance which you supplicate
Refuse I unreservedly to give.
Be governed by more sensible advice:
Exhaust the soothing, the placating arts
Of mild diplomacy; the central power invoke
Envoys t' accredit to a conference; 430
With view to your attaining an accord.
Throw out the grappling-hooks of compromise;
Take you the turning Caution points you to;
Grasp you the life-line Safety stretches you.
While not repenting of our steadfastness,
Our smitten federation in the past
Purchased, through rash unsheathing of the sword,
Of pain—of anguish—an eternity.
Had we election made th' Oneidas did,
During the late convulsions, brother, then, 440
No mocking memories of pleasant paths
Once trod; of fertile fields once tended—reaped—
Would now our waking thoughts employ; our joys
Diminish, and our peace disturb; no glimpse
Of devastated, blackened homes would our

Imagination haunt—our dreams oppress:
No Marah, with its rinseless after-taste
Of fallen fortunes—ruined prospects—would
Offensive contact with our lips have known.

*[Exeunt omnes.*

SCENE 9.—PLACE: *Upper Canada—The Highway, Burlington Heights.*

TIME: *Circ. 1800.*

Rushes upon THAYENDANEGEA, walking towards the Heights' hostelry, his son ISAAC—liquor-crazed—with brandished knife, and breathing sanguinary threats. In self-defence, THAYENDANEGEA is forced to meet his attack by using the small-sword of the British officer, which he always carried on his person. In the encounter the son is killed.

THAYENDANEGEA (*Solus*). To what accusing sacrilege has this 450
Paternal arm been driven? What act undreamt—
Atoneless—have I compassed? In what dread
Arena been th' impetuous, yet all
Unwilling actor? Shall I not inveigh
The fetid spring against of tragedy
So fearsome? Maledictions bitter I
Outpour upon that fangèd serpent—drink;
Ready accomplice, tool reliable

Of Satan; who, his wiles insidious
Practised afresh on victim pliable—  460
Caught at once more by mindless prey—him launched
On devious course; planted in fateful ways:
Helped—guided—hurried to appalling end.
Saddening enough the thought that reasoning soul
Should make surrender abject—kneel a slave—
To that dishonoring, that slakeless thirst,
Which man so often woos; to instinct gross
He stubbornly asserts to work his own
Undoing.  But for Isaac—him my first-
Born—of all beings sentient linked with this  470
Broad planet; but for him, my cherished and
Close image, thus enchained—embruted; whilst
Owning that spur malign, against whose power
Fought I a life-crusade—to blindly spend
On *this* fond frame his baleful rage; o'er *me*
To poise disgraceful dart; in *me* to choose
The object for unhallowed, callous blow!
Still, were there not repellent memories—
Portents, alas, full sinister—to preach  479
Forewarning of this luckless, this unnerving hour?
Had not a dismal, harsh experience
Given cogent cause to be prepared for such
Forbidding, ghastly scene?  In days agone
(Four lustres since *that* hapless contact) when

My sum of years enabled to oppose
An even strength to his mad onset, it
Became my wretched, my abhorrèd lot
To meet assault as frenzied—struggle know
As desperate : strife springing from the same
Inflaming source ; strife fathered by the same    490
Resistless impulse. Then ordained, as now,
Strait most unkind—trial most sore—to ward
Unfilial stroke ; combat a might, which well-
Nigh overwhelmed me ; which the target grazed
Of its perverted purpose. But to-day—
When that corrosive time, unchecked, bestows
Its blemishes ; (demon compassionless !)
Hastes to impress its ravages : when age
Disables with its wounds ; no longer now
Postpones invasion of the fibres ; doth    500
Palsy the muscles, and the sap dilute,
The natural forces could I not array
So as to stem that rush infuriate—
Th' unaided powers sufficed not to beat back
The vigorous, the deadly thrust. And so
This knife ; though guiltless of intent
Its self-loathed, stricken wielder (threatened was
My own slow-pulsing life by dint of that
Most vehement and straining close) evoked,
In blood, sequence irreparable. Can naught    510

Avail to temper the remorse; assuage
The tumult in this grief-charged breast?
How should these clutchers at my vitals—grim,
Relentless Typhons, flogging Furies, be bought off?
These robbers of my peace mainprized? When shall
Surcease be had for this wild agony?
Be raised for me dispiteous Torture's siege?

                      [*Exit* THAYENDANEGEA.

# EXPLANATORY NOTES.

## NOTES TO ACT I.

LINE 1.—"Onguiaahra." One of the many variants for the name of the "Falls" and river having vogue at the time. It is the form used by Lalemant in his *Relation des Hurons*. The stress should be laid on the penult, which approximates to the sound of *aw* in "law."

LINES 8-10; 15, 16.—A guttering discontent—the outcome, often, of discrepant causes in particular colonies—not seldom flaring up into actual insubordination, was rife among the inhabitants of certain of the eastern and sea-board Provinces even before the period of the French conquest.

LINE 17.—"Of the silk-woven banner both emit." The flag of the Bourbons exhibited for its device a triad of golden fleurs-de-lis, on a field of white samite.

LINE 36.—"Gael's second-sight vouchsafed me for the nonce." Many of the Scotch Highlanders arrogate the faculty of looking into the future; while the regular appearance of a family spectre, who comes to foretell approaching disaster or death, may, with confidence, be predicated. A striking example of this is furnished us in the case of Major Duncan Campbell, of the Black Watch. Several years before he joined the 42nd, while in his Castle of Inverawe, he had a vision. The wraith of his cousin Donald, whose murderer he had unwittingly sworn to shelter, thrice appeared to him; upon the last occasion pronouncing the doomful words: "Farewell, Inverawe; farewell, till we meet at TICONDEROGA!" The strange name dwelt in Campbell's memory; and when, in the year 1758, while serving under Abercromby, he was ordered to the attack upon Ticonderoga, he became instantly possessed with the gloomy certainty that death there awaited him. When the fortress was reached, his brother officers, aware of his superstitious fears, endeavored to relieve his mind by assuring him that they had not yet come to the fatal spot, but were then at Fort George. On the morning of the attack, Campbell came to them, with haggard face, saying: " I have seen him ! You have deceived me ! He came to my tent last night ! This is Ticonderoga ! I shall die to-day !" The prediction was fulfilled, as he received his death-wound in the ensuing engagement.

LINES 38-45.—The author would have scrupled to allow this image (caviare to the general) to be evoked by a *civilian*.

LINES 46-8.—Dramatic exigencies occasion a slight departure from fact, in indicating a meeting, *as though for the first time*, of the two commanders at Niagara. Johnson joined Prideaux at Oswego.

LINES 48-52.—Sir William Johnson, as yet an untitled Colonel of Militia, when he arrived at Lake George (known previously to the French as *Lac St. Sacrement*) changed, on the eve of the struggle, its designation to that which it has since borne ; choosing the sovereign's name in order to proclaim his territorial supremacy.

LINES 58-63.— Sir William Johnson, as stated in the foregoing note, was at this time an inexperienced militia-man.

LINES 69-75.—General Prideaux succeeded George Augustus, third Viscount Howe (older brother of Admiral Lord Howe, of "glorious first of June" fame, and of General Sir William Howe) as Colonel of the 55th Regiment of the line. Howe was killed, while bravely leading an assault against the French, near a point on the west side of the narrow channel, by which access is had to Lake George from the north, called Rogers' Rock. The battle of the 8th September, 1755, was fought at its southern extremity.

LINE 87.—T(*h*)ayendanegea. The accent is on the penult. Morgan spells it Ta-yen-da-na-ga. He was born in 1742.

LINE 89.—The author has, in a minor detail, deviated from history, by representing that Hendrick was shot down *before Johnson's eyes*. He lost his life, in reality, in the preliminary conflict, which was precipitated by an attempt to discover the lurking-place of the French. Thayendanegea was with the Mohawk auxiliaries under Hendrick.

LINE 115.—"To blossom into an academy." Colonel Ephraim Williams, on his way to Lake George, tarried at Albany to make his will; by which he conveyed the bulk of his estate to trustees to found a seat of learning; trammelling the grant only with the condition that it should bear his name. The academy was, in course of time, erected; and perpetuates its founder's memory in the present Williams College, at Williamstown, Mass.

LINES 133, 4.—Bradstreet, by a dashing descent made from the interior of the colony (New York) had captured Fort Frontenac during the previous summer.

LINES 135, 6.—"By whom La Corne's blind dash has just been foiled." The news of this unpleasant check for the French had been brought but a few days before.

LINE 151.—Sir William Johnson has been made use of to propagate the judgment of a number of military critics, concerning Pitt's plan of campaign, ventilated at the moment of the programme's being evolved.

LINES 165-9.—The work of the English engineers in building the initial approaches had been so defective as to call for unsparing animadversions from General Prideaux.

LINE 179.—"Sonnontouans." The French name for the Senecas.

LINE 229.—"Did I not battle for you frequently?" The speaker was pressing on the envoys' notice the French victories at Oswego, in 1756, the second affair of Fort William Henry in 1757, and Ticonderoga in 1758; when French—he with them—and Iroquois fought side by side. Captain Pouchot was a man of marked ability; and was the chief military engineer of the French throughout the campaigns; building, strengthening, and renovating—in addition to the defensive works at Lévis—the greater number of their forts, including Fort Niagara, a fact to which he refers in lines 430-2.

LINES 266-72.—"Missisakes." The French name for the Missisagas.

LINES 273-88.—"Poutéotamies." The French name for the Pottawatomies.

LINE 274.—"Isle." The Indians' appellative for America.

LINE 314.—The author would defy the most studious, untiring investigator to locate with certainty *La Belle Famille*. Parkman says the subsequent collision with the French relief-force occurred there. If this be so, it seems curious that Pouchot should have accepted without challenge the declaration of the Indians that they, *in the capacity of neutrals*, proposed transferring themselves to the point which he must have known was the one most likely to be chosen for what could not fail to have been regarded by him as an inevitable, as it promised to be an early, encounter. In the French commandant's memoirs there is at least one reference, which leaves it in doubt whether the elusive site was not on the *west* bank of the river.

LINE 320.—The fort called "Little Niagara," about a mile and a half south, on the portage from the Falls. Being pronounced untenable, Chabert was directed by Pouchot to burn it, and, with its inmates, proceed to Fort Niagara.

LINES 322.—The most intimate idea which was then vouchsafed to the aboriginal understanding touching the peculiar economy—the salient properties—of bombs was unbosomed by their comparing those death-dealing agents to "hot kettles."

LINES 384-90.—This incident, as well as the remainder of those which expose the internal proceedings of the French, is historical; and has been transcribed, with trifling variation or gloss, from Pouchot's memoirs of the siege.

LINES 421-4.—The "Dict. of Nat'l Biog." (art. on Prideaux) affords this information. The author has been unable to confirm it by allusions of any other authority, except McMullen.

LINES 443, 4.—"Ile de Marine." Navy Island.

LINE 455,—Pouchot's memoirs demonstrate, beyond the

admission of a doubt, that the battle with the relief-force was fought *somewhere* within the limits comprised by the clearing. Pouchot was enabled to see, though indistinctly, the manœuvres from the fort, as the text discloses; while it cannot be questioned that the open space did not extend, southerly from the fort, for more than two miles at the outside. Dr. Kingsford says that the fight occurred *nine* miles above the fort; and it is this assertion which induced the author to invite attention to the conditions tending to support the theory adopted in the text.

LINE 467.—By reason of the obscurity in which the situation of *La Belle Famille* would seem to be involved, the portage-outlet has been risked as a sufficiently definite statement of locality.

LINE 503.—The exertions made to balance the tireless activity—combat the potent intrigue—of the Jesuits were put forth, of course, by Johnson himself; but the author preferred that he should not self-satisfiedly trumpet his own achievements.

LINES 523, 4.—Massey, *as a regular*, had the right of succession.

LINE 552.—"Presqu' Ile." Now Erie, Penn.

LINE 553.—"Fort Machault and Le Bœuf." Now Franklin (the old Venango of the English) and Waterford, Penn., respectively.

FRAMEWORK OF SCENE 7.—The author volunteers the confession that he has done violence to history in putting Sir William Johnson in the trenches. Major Farquhar discharged the function of watch-dog in this connection; but, not wishing to sacrifice the item altogether, the author thought he would be pardoned for not importing a fresh character into the play, merely for the purpose of delivering the eight or ten lines needed to commemorate it. As a result of the battle, not announced in the verse, the two French Commanders, Aubry and De Ligneris, were, with a large number of their command, taken prisoners; the fort, in addition, being compelled to surrender.

## NOTES TO ACT II.

LINE 59.—There was an Upper and Lower "Castle" of the Mohawks.

LINES 103-6.—These companion services, one of which is preserved in the old Mohawk Church, near Brantford, and the other in the family of Dr. Oronhyatekha (whose wife is a great-grand-daughter of Brant) are models of artistically chased silver. Engraved on the flagon of each set is this inscription: "A.R. 1711. The gift of Her Majesty, Ann, by the grace of God, of Great Britain, France and Ireland, and of her plantations in North America, Queen, to her Indian chappel of the Mohawks."

LINE 107.—The speech which constitutes the foundation for this scene affords such striking testimony of the polemical ability of Thayendanegea; it illustrates so strongly his native clearness of reasoning—argues his possession of so large a fund of logical acumen—that it had been proposed to to insert it *in extenso*; but circumstances have rendered a curtailment of the notes absolutely necessary. The thought enwrapped in the lines 113-6 inclusive was, in substance, expressed.

LINE 150.—"The younger Livingston." William Livingston, who became the First Governor of New Jersey, under the new dispensation soon after inaugurated.

LINE 172.—Monckton was not Governor Tryon's *immediate* predecessor.

LINE 261.—Brant had summarily put down a rising of the Delawares in 1764, which, unchecked—the faggot having felt the flame kindled the preceding year by Pontiac—would, undoubtedly, have been fraught with serious consequences for the English. The conflagration blazed out afresh, when, a few months afterwards, the Shawanese formed an offensive alliance with the Delawares; but was quickly extinguished by Colonel Bouquet.

## EXPLANATORY NOTES.

LINE 281.—"Who planned to train my mind's crude faculties?" Thayendanegea, with several other Indian lads, had been sent by Sir William Johnson to Moor's Indian school, at Lebanon, Conn.; to whose principal, Dr. Eleazar Wheelock, Johnson—having himself profoundly at heart their temporal and spiritual welfare—extended warm and unwavering sympathy in all his efforts towards the enlightenment of the Indians. The school was later transferred to Hanover, N.H., and its name changed to Dartmouth College, which appellation it bears to-day. In after years, two of Brant's sons received their education in the same institution, under the guidance of Dr. Wheelock's son, who succeeded his father in the presidency of the college. Although originally an Indian mission school, whites do not appear to have been excluded, since Brant numbered among his school-fellows several of European stock.

LINES 287-303.—Brant had vainly petitioned Mr. Stuart to marry him to his deceased wife's half-sister.

LINE 304.—The work of translating the Scriptures into Mohawk, upon which Brant and the Rev. John Stuart were then engaged, had, perforce, on the part of the former, to be laid aside for more bellicose pursuits. When peace was restored, Thayendanegea resumed the work by himself; unaided, translating anew St. Mark's Gospel, and portions of the Book of Common Prayer, as well as preparing a useful primer.

LINE 311. — "Into your Canienga the chaste text." Canienga, Kanienga, Kanyungeh stand, in the Indian philology, for Mohawk.

LINE 325.—Johnstown was founded by Sir William Johnson.

LINE 340.—"Sacked the Chief Justice' sightly residence." Thomas Hutchinson was at this time Chief Justice.

LINES 363-82.—The episode of the Whately letters, with the complications it occasioned, forms one of the most memorable occurrences of the epoch. Sir William's last words prematurely record the exact fate of the petition.

LINES 397-9.—How strangely parallel seem the cases of Sir William Johnson and the chivalrous Montrose. The latter's original lines, through which are breathed such lofty decision —such unconquerable purpose—may be appropriately cited :

> "He either fears his fate too much, or his deserts are small,
> That dares not put it to the touch, to win or lose it all."

LINE 404.—The "Royal Grant." This gift was spontaneously bestowed upon Johnson by the Indians—an outward and visible sign of the great esteem in which they held him, the undisguised affection which they felt for him. It afterwards received the necessary ratification by the king.

LINE 410.—"My son's endowing with the accolade." The circumstance of Sir John Johnson's attaining the distinction of knighthood involves an interesting point. At the time of his father's being created a baronet, the rule decreed that the eldest son of a person so honored became, on reaching maturity, a knight. The provision was not abrogated until the beginning of the century.

LINES 435-41.—It is proper to be observed here that Sir William Johnson was at the same time the most extensive land-owner and the most opulent inhabitant of the colony.

LINE 497.—"Th' immortal treaty with the Senecas." This important treaty, made in 1764, gave Great Britain the ownership of a strip of land, four miles in width, on either side of the Niagara River—the concession embracing all the islands, as well—between the Falls and Lake Erie.

LINE 498.—The Fort Stanwix treaty, concluded in 1768, determined the western boundary between the territory of the settlers and Indians.

LINES 505, 6.—One of his biographers has applied the term "heaven-born general"—a characterization, doubtless, first bestowed upon Clive after Plassey—to Sir William Johnson.

LINE 547.—Sir William Johnson had united himself, according to Indian sanctions, with Brant's sister Molly.

# EXPLANATORY NOTES.           167

LINE 560-5.—It is a noteworthy fact that it was through the loving solicitude of the Mohawks for Sir William Johnson that the recuperative qualities of the Springs at Saratoga became known to the world. Beholding the sufferings of their "Great Brother," the warriors, in August, 1767, with touching devotion, insisted upon bearing him—part of the way in a litter on their shoulders—to this famous spot, whose health-giving properties were well known to them.

LINES 577-9.—Sir William Johnson, during the currency of the French wars, gave refuge in his own stronghold of Fort Johnson, for weeks, to a number of the Bourbon King's soldiers; whose lives were endangered by the threatening posture of the Indians. To disabuse any mind of the impression that the Alpine height of eulogium, which might be thought to be descried through Major Butler's fluent superlatives, has been *unwarrantably* opened to view, the author is content to confide in—to rest on—the ministry of two accessories—the summing up which the younger Stone admits into his biography of Sir William Johnson, that "he was the greatest character of the age"; and the prefatory remarks of the editor of his "Conferences and Treaties:" "To the truly British soul, whose eyes are forced on every object that may affect his country; to the loyal heart which glows with warmth at the name of the honored and illustrious hero of these pages; to him who knows the valor, martial qualifications and political talents of that victorious general, this book will afford a pleasing entertainment."

LINES 606-8.—Massachusetts Bay—the gun-cotton crammed into the ordnance of the revolt—had just responded to the agitation at the touch-hole.

LINES 617-19.—The reference is to the statute directing a trial in England of those concerned in the ebullient Boston riots. The author would say, generally, that he has simply amplified the genuine heads of the argument addressed to the intemperate gathering by Colonel Johnson.

LINE 658.—The real contestant with Colonel Johnson on

this occasion was Jacob Sammons, the *son* of Sampson. The author considered, however, that it would be advisable to pit against the influence and weight in the community of Colonel Johnson a partizan not more inferior to him in standing and importance than it was practicable to procure; and, for this reason (the son, too, an unmoneyed, dependent young man of twenty-two being unlikely to enjoy the needful insight into the situation) imposed the burden of the emergency upon the father—as perfervid a "patriot," certainly, as his son. A project taken in hand by him for rescuing a political prisoner from gaol led to firing the first shot in New York.

LINES 663, 4.—The rebutting speech does not circumscribe itself to the case of New York; which, with Delaware and North Carolina, escaped *this* prohibition. Whether excusable procedure or not, there was embanked by the residents of one colony, exempted from their operation, a reservoir of sympathy with the oppression and wrongs imagined to be visited upon, or endured by another; repeated turnings on of the hydrants connecting with which it was impossible to resist.

## NOTES TO ACT III.

LINE 5.—"Macdonells with no paltry pedigree." A number of the Macdonells, accompanying Sir John Johnson in his flight to Canada, in 1776, joined their clansmen in Glengarry. The chief of one branch of the clan is Mr. John A. Macdonell, of Alexandria.

LINES 11-3.—Sir John did not, in reality, begin to fortify Johnson Hall until the winter.

LINES 19-22. —Alexander White, who was conspicuous for his Royalist proclivities; expressed through a chain of overt acts giving great umbrage to the colonials—the most grudgeenkindling of which was his uprooting of a "Liberty-Pole" in the German Flats.

# EXPLANATORY NOTES. 109

LINE 23.—In this, and in line 43, by the Council is meant the New York Assembly.

LINE 48.—Rev. Samuel Kirkland was chaplain to the Oneidas, and exercised an unbounded influence over them. His son became Principal of Harvard College.

LINE 90-2.—The precept, as it was recalled by his pupil to Dr. Wheelock, ran: "That they" (the boys) "might be able to live as good subjects, to fear God, and honor the King."

LINE 112.—Shonectady. One of the countless orthographic samples of the vocable which denotes the ancient city.

LINE 122.—"Warraghiyagey." The Indian name for Sir William Johnson. He had, for reasons which he regarded sufficient, resigned his post of Superintendent of Indian Affairs in 1751, and did not resume it till 1755.

LINE 179.—Sir Guy Carleton was known to be strongly averse to the employment of Indians; and had declined the aid of certain of the tribes, when he was required to meet Montgomery and Arnold's disturbing invasion.

LINE 205.—"Kora." Kora, Goragh—corruptions of Corlaer—was a title derived from the patronymic of a Dutch patroon in the Mohawk Valley, Arendt Van Corlaer, for whom the Iroquois entertained great reverence; and was given by them to the English Governors of Canada. The Queen of Great Britain is still called by many of the Indians " Kora-Kowa," or Chief Governor.

LINES 218-30.—The *verbatim* judgment of the chief in this connection (not delivered, however, until after the war) was, "I like the organ well, the harpsichord better; but the drum and trumpet best of all, for they make my heart beat quick."

LINE 313.—Whilst the author questions whether it can be *positively* established that Thayendanegea was not at this Council, the accounts we have of his movements at the time would seem to preclude the possibility of such being the case. He did not return from England until the beginning of August; and Capt. Cruikshank, in his pamphlet, "Joseph

Brant in the Revolution," declares that he fought in the battle of Long Island, at the end of the month. It likewise appears that while in New York he, in November, offered himself upon a mission to the Mohawk Valley. Nevertheless—since it can be averred beyond dispute that he attended a great many councils of the period—it has been thought that a dramatic license would sanction his being introduced at what was the most important Indian palaver of the day. The Indians' posture did not become irrevocable until the Council at Oswego in the following year.

LINE 374.—The trio of picturesque lakes in the Cayugas' country—Cayuga, Owasco and Skaneateles.

LINE 434.—The date of this meeting is shrouded in dubiety. Some authorities say the end of June; Campbell, in his "Annals of Tryon County"—an allegation this which Stone endorses—speaks of a fine July morning. The 4th of July has been selected for a reason sufficiently apparent.

LINES 440-52.—The ensign was not, in reality, unfurled until the commencement of the siege.

LINES 466-73.—The oral passages indulged are, as nearly as possible, in the language of the real altercation.

LINES 481-4.—The Trenton collision took place in the night between the 25th and 26th December, 1776, and that at Princeton in the night between the 1st and 2nd January, 1777.

LINE 510, 1.—"The fame transcendent of the Kennebec." The piercing by Arnold of the Kennebec wilderness has been compared to Napoleon's passage of the Simplon.

LINES 533-7.—Lafayette not only tendered his sword to Washington, but had placed at his disposal his large fortune.

LINES 554-63.—Herkimer solicited, as a *quid pro quo* for altered conduct towards the missionary, the surrender of some deserters; but the chief denied his request. Mr. Stuart was not allowed to leave until 1780.

LINE 566.—Hartwick's Grant. Now Cooperstown, at the southern extremity of Otsego Lake. There was, as a matter of fact, no proceeding by Herkimer, nor prior agreement entered into with Schuyler to proceed, to Hartwick's Grant. A pretext adequate enough to bring about an enlargement of the negotiations till the following day had, notwithstanding, to be found, in order to give Herkimer time to summon his accomplice; and lay in train the projected mine, of the groundwork of which the discussion carried on in the succeeding scene makes suitable disclosure. Cooperstown was founded, in 1786, by the father of J. Fenimore Cooper; and was the novelist's birth-place.

LINE 601.—As a conception lending itself to a more satisfactory evolution of the crisis, the author, as will be observed, imagines Waggoner—conscience-stung—to have resolved on notifying Thayendanegea of the machinations at work against him.

LINE 621.—This declaration was actually made, but not till after the war. It formed the answer of the Mohawks to a proposal from the Senecas that they should settle amonst them.

LINE 625.—The Six-Nations invariably called the insurgents "Bostonians."

FRAMEWORK OF SCENES 5 AND 7.—There has been, in handing down the transactions embodied in the interviews which form the bases for these two scenes, a close adherence to history. The only essential variation—a liberty resorted to by the author for the purpose of providing an inspiriting culmination to the act—lies in the conjuring up by the chief of the apparition of his dependents from the forest, on the occasion of the *resumed* debate with Herkimer. This intensely theatrical interruption of their parley took place on the *first* day. The sachem, having good ground to apprehend a display of bad faith, employed the precautionary measure of having his warriors within call.

LINE 643.—"How flourishes the exile?" Klock, by reason of his systematic misconduct, was forced to flee the country.

LINE 645.—The epithet used was even more scurrilous.

LINES 685-7.—Brant and Herkimer had, for several years, resided within three miles of each other. The situation was on the south side of the river near the present town of Danube.

LINES 712-4.—Thayendanegea turned out to be no fallible diviner; for the contingency signified through the words—those being historic—in which he couches his farewell greeting to Herkimer, drifted into verity.

## NOTES TO ACT IV.

LINE 5.—The entire course of the war would have been changed, had not Lord George Germain, who was at this time Secretary of State for the Colonies, been guilty of incredible negligence. "Lord George, having, among other peculiarities, a particular aversion to be put out of his way on any occasion, had arranged to call at his office, on the way to the country, in order to sign the despatches" (authorizing Howe to form a junction with Burgoyne) "but, as those addressed to Howe had not been 'fair copied'; and he was not disposed to be balked of his projected visit into Kent, they were not signed then, and were forgotten on his return to town." Lord E. Fitzmaurice's "Life of Lord Shelburne."

LINE 12.—Valcour was an island in Lake Champlain.

LINE 15.—St. Clair yielded the fort at the first summons.

LINE 22.—"The Great Carrying-Place." The short portage conducting from the source of the Mohawk, near Fort Stanwix, to Wood Creek, the eastern outlet of Oneida Lake; called, also, the Oneida, or Central Carrying-Place.

LINE 25.—"For this St. Leger bowls his scorching sleet." Brig.-Gen. Barry St. Leger commanded the besieging column before Fort Stanwix.

LINE 53.—"Those falls entrancing." The falls at Cohoes, reputed to be—before that Blue-Beard of utilitarianism, the Erie Canal, caused such extensive depletions of their volume,

# EXPLANATORY NOTES. 173

the most considerable, as they still are, the most beautiful, cascade in the State.

LINE 55.—"Those in miniature." The "little falls," in contradistinction to those at Cohoes. The town which stands on the southern margin of the Mohawk at this point bears the same name.

LINE 77.—Gansevoort is a word of three syllables.

LINES 79-84.—A moderate adulteration of error enters into this version. Molly Brant—who is thought by many to have possessed as great ability as her brother—was not the actual bearer of the message, but had commissioned an agile and trustworthy Mohawk to carry the intelligence from Canajoharie. The vicarious manner in which the service was performed does not seem to have in any way discounted its value in the eyes of the British Government; who, for this and other loyal acts, bestowed upon her an annuity of £100.

LINE 86.—"My home-bred rangers." Butler's Rangers can hardly be said to have existed as an independent organization at this early period. The close of the year, however, found them a full-ranked, powerful corps. They could not have been regulars, as their leader's name is absent from the army lists of the time.

LINE 133.—"To Major Watts, our sorest casualty." Major Watts was Sir John Johnson's brother-in-law; and had been sent forward by St. Leger, with a detachment of "Johnson's Greens," to reinforce Thayendanegea and Butler.

LINES 141-150.—There is an inversion of events—pardonable, it is hoped—confessed through these lines. Brant's command, after the action at Oriskany, chastised the Oneidas for acts of troublesome hostility perpetrated during the field-operations; and the Oneidas, as soon as the chieftain's back was turned, revenged themselves on his defenceless sister and her family.

LINES 158-66.—General Herkimer died as the consequence of an amputation of his wounded leg. A monument has been erected at his burial place—the grave being on the estate he owned when his life was so tragically cut short.

FRAMEWORK OF SCENE 3.—The author has met with serious difficulty in bringing the principal actors in this scene together, without a too flagrant flying in the face of history. Stone declares that the affair transpired at the "Cedars" on May 18th, 1776. It cannot be questioned that *Captain McKinstry* attended there; but as Thayendanegea addressed the British Secretary of State, in person, on the 7th of May of that year, touching certain claims and grievances of his tribe; and, moreover—having sailed from England—did not arrive at Staten Island until the 5th of *August*, the hypothesis of their meeting at the "Cedars" need not be further canvassed. A localizing of the encounter at Oriskany was next adventured; but the author here found himself confronted, in cold-blooded fashion, with the roster of Provincial officers who participated in that engagement, in which McKinstry's name did not appear. Captain Cruikshank (who has been proved to be a fruitful burrower) having placed Brant at Saratoga, a fixing of the event during the contact at Stillwater apparently selects the least assailable position which was open to be assumed. The author feels convinced that Thayendanegea, after *some* battle during the Revolution, interposed to save his whilom friend from a death by torture; for the latter, at the conclusion of the war, showed him peculiar consideration by reason of the preservation so wrought. Ackland was in command of the Grenadiers. It is the purest conjecture of the author that his officers might have pooled their shillings to help purchase the ox.

LINE 214.—" Weston, swift-mustering quota of the guard." Colonel Weston, or Wesson, was the commandant at Fort Dayton (now Herkimer) in the German Flats.

LINE 275.—Speaking of this incident Stone says: "The eloquence and pathos with which she Mary (?) Schuyler pleaded for the life of her son, were long remembered in the

# EXPLANATORY NOTES. 175

unwritten history of the Mohawk Valley." Mrs. Schuyler (whose baptismal name Benton's "Herkimer County" gives as *Elizabeth Barbara*) was a sister of General Herkimer. To be accurate, Schuyler was sentenced to death before his mother poured forth her supplication; but—hostile fact so rearing its stockade—the gymnast's flexileness was borrowed to leap the pales. The author, with respect to the latitude here taken, as well as in the matter of a few similar deflections, begs to be forgiven for letting dramatic license, as it were, unwind the tourniquet which history beneficially employs to check the would-be instructor's flow of unreliable or dubious statement.

LINES 296-8.—"This seeming simpleton claims veneration," etc. It may not be generally known that the unenlightened savage invests the demented amongst themselves, as well as the whites, with supernatural gifts. In reproducing the court-martial scene, and the *ruse de guerre* to which the proceedings gave birth, there has been a conscientious consulting of the claims of history.

FRAMEWORK OF SCENE 6.—Susan Campbell is herself a fictitious person, though there was a female delegate, or delegates, actually authorized to wait upon Colonel Alden. There was a numerous colony of Campbells in the settlement.

LINE 307.—A traveller in the East states that, owing to the great speed of the gazelle, it cannot be taken through the unassisted instrumentality of dogs. The falcon requires to be pressed into service; and of the mode of chase, onset, and capture our traveller presents a vivid picture. The gazelles having been sighted, the falcons are let loose. They immediately fasten themselves—each one upon the head of a separate animal—and by a vigorous flapping of their wings, and by pecking at the timid creature's eyes, soon reduce it to such a state of confusion that it becomes an easy prey for the hunters.

LINE 330.—It was in no small degree owing to the operations of this ingenious Oneida; who, engaging the assistance of several Indians of his acquaintance, used them as vehicles to spread the tidings throughout the camp, that such complete success attended Schuyler's enterprise.

LINES 366, 7.—Schuyler's coat, to aid the deception, had been riddled before leaving Fort Dayton.

LINE 381.—On the 8th of November, Colonel Alden had been warned that an attack by the Rangers and Indians was imminent, but had scouted the intelligence as an idle Indian rumor. He denied the solicitations of the people to be permitted to transport themselves and their effects to the fort, assuring them that their alarm was foundationless, and that his vigilant scouts would inform them of the first approach of danger.

FRAMEWORK OF SCENE 7.—The name of the female actor not having been preserved, that given her is an invention of the author. The true state of facts was that Thayendanegea, having persuaded the woman to feign illness, remained until after the departure of the Senecas; and was, by this expedient, able to divert their bloody purpose. He then—having first caused the intended victims to be marked with his totem, the sign of a wolf—withdrew. Coupled with many well-authenticated instances of Brant's having either conducted, or directed affrighted women to places of shelter, an incident narrated by Stone comports happily with one's notion of his considerateness. In 1780, a woman came to General Van Rensselaer—then having his headquarters at Fort Hunter—lamenting tearfully the loss of her infant, which had been snatched from the cradle. The next morning an Indian warrior bounded into the room where the General's officers were breakfasting, bearing an infant in his arms, and also a letter from Brant, addressed "to the commanding officer of the rebel army." The message, *inter alia*, contained these words: "Sir, I send you, by one of my runners, the child which he will deliver, that you may know that whatever others may do, *I* do not make war upon women and children."

## NOTES TO ACT V.

**FRAMEWORK OF SCENE 1.**—The incident here utilized is founded on undoubted fact. It should be noticed, however, in fuller elucidation of the occurrence, that the claimant for protection and relief practised a shameless imposture upon the chief, which was not discovered until afterwards. He was not, in truth, a Freemason at all; yet had, in some unaccountable manner, got hold of the distress-signal. Brant, though highly incensed over the perpetration of the fraud, did not alter his conduct towards the delinquent. There are other instances of Thayendanegea's having saved, during the war, the lives of persons, who either claimed, or were known, to belong to the craft.

**FRAMEWORK OF SCENE 2.**—The Lieutenant Harper introduced was an ancestor of the proprietors of *Harper's Monthly*.

**LINES 82-95.**—Brant-goose—a species of wild goose. The chief learnt of this challenge; but at a time when it was inconvenient to gratify the longings of its gasconading publisher.

**LINES 122-7.**—Harper, to shield the settlement from attack, palmed off a mendacious story upon Brant. There were, as a fact, no regulars in any of the three forts.

**FRAMEWORK OF SCENE 3.**—The author has, in this and scene 4, capriciously identified John Mohawk (the name given by Simms, in his "Frontiersmen of New York," to the survivor of the tragedy) with Canastota. He is free to admit that—to assimilate the tale of the four savages having been dispatched by a *single* discharge of Pence's rifle—his credulity has been taxed in as rare degree, as that of most of his readers is bound to be. The account, however, is solemnly vouched for by Simms; being supplemented only by supposing the Indians to have been so couched before the fire as to render the issue a trifle less improbable.

**LINE 215.**—"To spiteful buffets from the gauntlet-files."

To have secured the prisoners' *absolute* immunity from this distressing ordeal was beyond the chief's power.

FRAME-WORK OF SCENE 7.—The precise attitude assumed by Brant in connection with the north-western disturbance, is not easy to be arrived at; though he seems, at first, to have favored a recourse to energetic means to bring the thirteen colonies to terms; subsequently, however, receding from that position. Stone says that he took part in the battle in which St. Clair sustained such a calamitous defeat; but the author, noting the slender fabric of testimony upon which his assertion rests—some misty tradition in the family—boldly impugns its correctness. Campbell, in his "Travels in North America"—published in 1793—reports that he paid a visit of several days to the chief, in the winter (1792) following the disaster. Some of the reflections indulged between them have a vital bearing on this speculation. He says, "At the same time, I am convinced that he" (Brant) "bears no good will to the American States; *and seems to be much rejoiced at the drubbing their troops got from the Indians on the 4th of last November.*" Will any candid intelligence maintain that this is the sort of reception of the subject which would have been attested by one who figured *in propriâ personâ* in the fray? Again, when toasts were proposed: "Our first toasts were King, Queen, and Prince of Wales; and, next, *to the brave fellows who drubbed the Yankees;* all given by the *landlord* in regular progression." Does an individual, as a rule, join others in drinking—let alone pledge—his own health in a toast?

LINE 265.—"As those their offshoots by St. Lawrence found." The Caughnawagas and St. Regis, who many years before had removed to the banks of the St. Lawrence, and bore the appellation of the "seventh nation."

LINE 283.—"Retains in pawn th' outlying fortresses." Michillimackinac (Mackinaw) Oswegatchie (Ogdensburg) Niagara, Oswego, and Presqu' Ile.

LINE 329.—"As one deep-learned in warfare's subtleties."

# EXPLANATORY NOTES.

In addition to the pitched battles which have been depicted, or touched upon in the text, Brant headed his Indians in the memorable combat with General Sullivan at the Chemung, in 1779; besides participating in several furious shocks—a number of sharp scrimmages—during Sir John Johnson's irruptions in 1780.

LINE 351.—"Of my face-pigment's being a true vermeil." The ambassador fancied the chieftain wore a mask, while he was merely plentifully smudged with paint.

LINE 378.—"Long-Knives." A title given by the Indians to the whites.

LINE 483.—A modern romance, entitled "Bart the Hunter," relates that Brant was set upon in the same way by his son during the Revolutionary War. It should be added that there is a conflict of evidence as to whether the homicidal horror happened within doors, or in the open air. Lord Dorchester refused to accept the surrender of Brant's sword—proffered to him immediately after its commission.

FRAMEWORK OF SCENE 9.—The author, impelled by a dramatic necessity, has represented the son's death as having been immediate, whereas the injury inflicted was not, *in itself*, fatal. The victim, in the unhinged condition to which he had been brought through indulgence in his habit, tore off the bandages which had been applied to the wound, thereby superinducing erysipelas. The author, anticipating the objection that the dramatic unities are but questionably subserved by his using this scene as the climax to the play, hopes, by a casual reminder, to weaken its force. For his excuse—if excuse be needed—for introducing it, he trusts to the terrific irony which was involved in the fact of one, who had waged an unceasing warfare against the enthralling curse of his people's addiction to liquor, becoming even the approximate cause of the death of his own son, whilst that son was under its influence,

www.ingramcontent.com/pod-product-compliance
Lightning Source LLC
Chambersburg PA
CBHW032152160426
43197CB00008B/873